EXECUTRIX

THE SUE WILLIAM SILVERMAN PRIZE

FOR CREATIVE NONFICTION

EXECUTRIX

BRITTANY PERHAM

THE UNIVERSITY OF GEORGIA PRESS *Athens*

This book is the winner of the 2025 Sue William Silverman Prize for Creative Nonfiction, part of the Association of Writers & Writing Programs (AWP) Award Series. AWP is a nonprofit organization dedicated to amplifying the voices of writers and the academic programs and organizations that serve them. Please visit www.awpwriter.org for more information.

Published by the University of Georgia Press
Athens, Georgia 30602
www.ugapress.org

Designed by Katrina Noble
Set in Scala
Printed and bound by Sheridan Books
The paper in this book meets the guidelines for permanence and durability of the Committee on Production Guidelines for Book Longevity of the Council on Library Resources.

Printed in the United States of America
30 29 28 27 26 P 5 4 3 2 1

EU Authorized Representative
Easy Access System Europe—Mustamäe tee 50, 10621 Tallinn, Estonia, gpsr.requests@easproject.com

Library of Congress Control Number: 2026938228
ISBN: 9780820377780 (paperback)
ISBN: 9780820377797 (epub)
ISBN: 9780820377803 (PDF)

ACKNOWLEDGMENTS

Thank you to the Civitella Ranieri Foundation, the Hemingway House, Vermont Studio Center, and Yaddo for giving me time to write this book. Thank you to the editors of *Prairie Schooner* and *Tupelo Quarterly*, in which sections of this book first appeared. Thank you to Cheryl Strayed and to everyone at AWP and UGA Press who made this book possible. Thank you to Kim Addonizio, Jan Beatty, Harriet Clark, Jennifer Foerster, Sarah Frisch, M. Gessen, Charlotte Gordon, Ben Gucciardi, Tom Kealey, Scott Laughlin, Julia Loktev, Peter Mann, Randall Mann, Lauren Markham, Kate Petersen, Kirstin Valdez Quade, Rakesh Satayal, Sarah Schweig, Matthew Siegel, Susan Steinberg, Elizabeth Tallent, Elizabeth Winthrop, and Marya Zilberberg. Thank you, first and last, to Peter Kline. This book is for Cameron Perham and for Leigh Perham, who gave me their stories and believed this one.

EXECUTRIX

The Death Story

My father is dying and I have no notebook. When it's over, I'll regret this.

He's dying right now behind the curtain. They're removing all the pieces.

13:37:37 scrolls on the LED screen over the hallway where I'm standing. I'll remember this later because I think, you'll remember this later.

There are three of them in there. One is the Nurse, one is the Respiratory Therapist, one is my father. Behind the curtain, I can see their shadows and the shadows of the machines standing around the shadow of the bed. In other units, there are no windows, but in here there are. Beyond the curtain and the shadows, it's a sunny day.

My brother and I are out here. We're standing near some computer screens. Behind the nurses' station, a few people do small things, telephone keyboard clipboard.

When these people walk by, they give us the distance they've been taught to give us. They don't look at us the way people look at crying people on the street. Instead, they just walk by. Maybe for a while they tried to comfort each family before they learned to keep walking. Maybe they were reprimanded so they learned.

They walk into other rooms with other families. We are not their family.

We are the family of this one Nurse behind the curtain. As soon as I leave here, I won't remember her name and I'll wish I did. She speaks at an appropriate volume. She expresses sorrow without feeling it.

My father might already be dead because his brain shows no activity. But I'm unclear on this point because his body is, at least for the next few minutes, sort of alive in there.

My brother and I have had the Doctor conversation already. It took about ten minutes. Doctor Nurse Social Worker sat in a row opposite us in the ICU conference room. Maybe they practice this in school. They are told not to show impatience sadness confusion. They are told to speak in clear succinct sentences and to sit still under questioning. Under no circumstances should they cry. I don't blame them at all.

Doctor said, his brain shows no activity. Doctor said, brainstem. I wrote some things down on the back of my boarding pass.

Brain Brainstem Braindeath

Extubation Breath stop Heart stop

How long does it take?

We're notoriously bad at predicting this, Doctor said. We don't think it will take long.

We have just this last question, we said.

We're notoriously bad at predicting this, Nurse said. It probably won't be long.

I said I didn't think there was a reason to wait. I'd been flying all night and my father was gone already. I said "gone" although I would've rather said "dead" because I don't like the terms "gone" or "passed" or "crossed over." Those metaphors make me feel uncomfortable. But I said "gone" to make Doctor Nurse Social Worker feel more comfortable. And because I wasn't sure if the word "gone" would make my brother feel more comfortable than the word "dead." If metaphors make him feel more comfortable, I can get behind them.

Social Worker asked us if we wanted a chaplain to deliver the sacrament of the sick. Then she said, something something we're all just so sorry. Then she looked like she would cry. I directed all my anger sadness confusion at her because her job is to sit there every day without crying.

No thank you; we have no tradition in this case.

Social Worker said, I can help you arrange for a funeral home to collect the remains.

No, we said.

Later I'll regret saying, I've been flying all night. Later I'll feel ashamed.

At the end of the interview, Nurse said my brother and I could be in the room or not when it happened. She did not say "death" nor what "it" signified though "it" was or would end in "death." It was up to us. Different people choose different things, she said. If we didn't choose to be there, she would be there, so he wouldn't be alone.

I was and am unclear on this point: If he was already dead, how would he be alone?

My brother and I didn't want him to be alone, dead or alive, without us.

Yes, we said.

We're ready, they said. Doctor Nurse Social Worker stood up from the conference table. We stood up from the conference table. Good luck, Doctor said. I'm sorry for your loss, Social Worker said. Whenever you're ready, Nurse said. There's no reason to wait, I said. I wondered how long we'd have to wait.

My father's been without us a lot already.

In hospitals you can wait a long time.

But they didn't make us wait. Maybe it's protocol in these cases. They've been taught to get on it as soon as you say go. So Nurse said, stand right here in the hall just for a moment. We have a few things to prepare.

We stand right here in this hall just for the moment. Then Nurse and Respiratory Therapist come back to our side of the curtain. Respiratory Therapist doesn't talk to us because she's been trained not to talk to us. Then Nurse takes us over to the other side.

We don't know how long it will take now.

Nurse says, we're notoriously bad at predicting this. Doctor said, we're notoriously bad at predicting this. Social Worker said, we're all just so sorry.

We've been told to expect gasping and gurgling. Sometimes it happens, sometimes it doesn't.

We haven't been told that the death certificate will read, "END STAGE LIVER DISEASE due to (or as a consequence of) ALCOHOLIC CIRRHOSIS." Later this will surprise us even though we know it to be accurate.

Nurse says, I don't expect him to take a breath on his own, but we're bad at predicting this.

This is because brain death has traveled from the brain to the brainstem and even the most basic brain functions shouldn't be working anymore. This is what they think.

We're all here on this side of the curtain. Here is my father, and here is my brother, and here I am. My father's body is not attached to anything anymore. The respirator and the infusion pumps wait around the bed like ownerless dogs, all their leashes dropped on the floor.

The monitors have been turned off. Nothing will beep or alarm. You won't be disturbed, Nurse says.

When Nurse leaves, it's unclear to me if my father is breathing. I can see the pulsebeat in his neck and the heartbeat in his chest.

I have one hand on my brother's hand, which is on my father's hand, which is cartoon-large.

It's unclear to me if there are two or three of us in this room.

I can see far inside my father's mouth and all the brown borders of his teeth. I can see better now than I could earlier, when the breathing tube and the feeding tube were taking up a lot of space.

I'm glad there's a window looking out between wings of the hospital at Storrow Drive, then the Esplanade, then the Charles River.

I have one hand on my father's shoulder underneath the gown. Here is my father's shoulder.

It takes a second and then the color of his face changes. The color change starts from his forehead and draws down smoothly like the window shade on an airplane.

The new color is a color I've never seen before so there are no comparisons.

There's one white tree out there and a man with a Labrador. Later I'll be interested to know what tree it is that makes those white flowers days before any of the other trees are even budding.

This color thing is the most shocking thing.

This is the only city where I knew my father and that was a long time ago.

The most shocking thing.

Pulsebeat heartbeat. Breath? Redbud? Cherry blossom?

I'm glad to see that what's going on in here isn't going on out there for the man and the dog. For a minute I imagine I'm the dog with the tennis ball in my mouth.

I'm unclear about the breath situation. Did he take a breath or is this just the heart still going? This is something I'll forget to ask and later I'll wish I had.

His usually large bottom lip is unusually large.

On the wall is a whiteboard that lists some things you'd expect:

Patient's Name: ______________
Date: ______________
Room Number: ______________
Goals for the Day: ______________
Expected Discharge Date: ______________

Nurse said she'll come in to tell us when his heart stops. So really we're waiting for her.

All of the blanks are blank, even Patient's Name: ______________.

Now I get myself ready to talk to my father. For the first few minutes this is hard to do. I say things like (1) the moment of transition is the hardest moment; (2) we will be connected in a new way; (3) we love you.

I don't know if I'm speaking for my brother or to my brother, to my father or for him. I don't know if platitudes are the only true things.

I say things like (4) it's getting cloudy but it's a pretty day; (5) we're looking out over the river and there's a white tree.

What would I want to hear if I could hear?

Then my brother says the first thing he's said to my father: I love you. What? I say, because I think my brother is speaking to me. Then no one says anything for a while.

My father would know the name of the tree because that's the kind of thing he knows (knew).

I'm unclear about how many of us are in this room.

I hope the things I'm saying are things my father knows (knew). But if I don't believe that the he-himself is anywhere as the he-himself, how will he know?

Nurse will come in to tell us when his heart stops. There is no gasping or gurgling. Just that color change, which is the disturbing thing.

I like to think of his energy going into the Great Big Energy That Knows Everything. That's the best I can do. And I don't believe "energy" or "knows" or "everything" are the appropriate words.

Now I have to watch the tears. My father is crying. I guess the tears have nowhere to go without the blinking so they just come out.

Before this part started, Nurse said she was giving him extra pain medicine, even though she was sure he wasn't feeling any pain. If she's sure he isn't feeling any pain, why give him extra pain medicine? Is this to make us feel better? Let me say this: It doesn't.

I take the tear from under his right eye and think about holy water even though I have no experience with holy water and holy water means nothing to me.

Nurse will come any minute now. Even though I have little experience with my father's face.

It's clear to me that I love my father and that I loved him all the years we went without speaking. This is not a revelation.

"Went without" is an appropriate phrase, as in "went without food." Now he is going without me. And: He has gone without me. And: I will go without him until I die too.

The wall clock says two-oh-five-in-the-afternoon. On a semi-cloudy day, in Boston, beside the Charles River.

Goodbye, we love you.

Later I'll hope that what I said meant something to someone in this room but I know it was disorganized and badly delivered. You could tell it was coming from someone who didn't know what she believed.

I'm unclear about a lot of things until Nurse comes in and says, his heart stopped.

Now we don't know what to do. Get out of there.

I'm outside the curtain before my brother is and Nurse asks if I want an autopsy. I say no even though who knows I don't know but I don't want my brother to have to decide one more thing. Later, when I tell him about this, he'll say he heard everything, and I'll write this down on a notepad I take from the funeral home. I who have been responsible for none of my father's stories will write his death story. I ask Nurse if there's anything else we need to do.

No.

So we just leave?

Yes.

What a Day!

In the hospital elevator, my brother and I are alone.

In the parking garage, the Dead Dads appear. Because I've made them up, I'm not surprised to see them. The two of them look just alike leaning against my brother's truck. They breathe in and out like synchronized swimmers. My brother is unlocking the doors.

Climb in, I say, and the Dead Dads are in the truck bed. Better than a hearse, I hear one of them say.

The truck circles down the down ramp.

In the street, a woman jumps out of a car saying, I cut my finger I cut my finger. She's holding up her finger. The guard directing traffic waves her toward the ER.

Someone's having a bad day, my brother says.

In my brother's truck, we ride through the city. The Dead Dads ride through the city in the bed of my brother's truck.

Both Dead Dads are wearing the clothes my father wore when I was a child. They each wear my father's sunglasses and my father's red Nautica jacket embroidered with an architectural drawing of a J Class yacht and the words "J Class Yacht." I can picture the words and the jacket exactly. My finger traces the lettering until my father's closet closes around me.

Both Dead Dads have my father's fat bottom lip and poorly shaved face. One of them has the sunglasses on, the red rubber strap pulled tight around his head the way my father used to do it. This one taps on the cab's glass. Faster, Buddy! he yells to my brother, who can't hear him because these are my Dead Dads. If my brother has his own Dead Dads, he hasn't mentioned it.

Just about sailing weather again, this Dead Dad yells to me. The Charles River appears at the end of Charles Street. The salt-and-pepper bridge, I say, and the two of us look across the water and remember when I was little and liked to count the saltshakers. He gives me the thumbs up. Good Dad-in-the-Sky.

That name makes me sound like a puppy, he says, or a Jack-in-the-Box. But I'll take it.

The other Dead Dad is holding the tailgate to keep himself upright. He's disappearing inside his jacket. A snail caught too far above the tideline, is what I think. Then I think, maudlin. His face is my father's death face.

I was dying, he says. Where were you?

Bad Dead Dad.

The two Dead Dads: The angel and the devil in Saturday morning cartoons? This is the form I've given them and now I'm stuck with it.

Good Dad-in-the-Sky is growing a full beard and getting big as my childhood daddy. The jacket's tight across his fat belly. He pounds on the glass with his big fist. Faster! he says. What a day!

My brother drives toward the Common. I think of telling him about the Dead Dads: One looks like Dad when we were kids, and one looks like that dead body back there. They're both sitting in the bed of your truck. Fanfuckingtastic, my brother might say.

What a day, my brother says.

Good Dad-in-the-Sky pounds on the glass. I wish the window would open so I could hear you guys better, he says.

Before We Begin

I have to tell you I don't know this story. There are things I don't remember. I wanted to find out something about my father and here we are.

I have to tell you not much changes between the beginning and the end. I don't know and then I don't know.

I have to tell you there was no trauma, don't even say that word. I wasn't raped or beaten or turned out of the house. Don't expect anything good.

I have to tell you I don't always understand the characters, their actions, or to whom the actions should be ascribed. For example, I don't know why my father and I didn't speak for ten years until he was almost dead. For example, I don't know if it's more accurate to say, I don't know why *I didn't speak to my father* for ten years.

Until he was almost dead is accurate.

I have to tell you not much changes between the beginning and the end. Don't expect a good ending. For example, I did not climb a mountain, take an international trip, find a new lover, learn cooking baking home repair or any new skill. I did not survive a plane crash, an addiction, or the wilderness, and I did not triumph over any odds. Let's just get that out of the way right now.

And actually I did some of those things. I have to tell you they're the ones you'd expect.

I have to tell you I hate those notes to the reader in the front of memoirs that say, "I have sometimes re-created conversations, condensed characters, or left out nonessential characters or scenes."

Because what, everything else is true?

To that I have to say, fuck you. I have to tell you, a lot of this is made up. There is no other way.

I have to tell you this story is informed by lots of other stories, the stories I've been told and the stories I've told myself. How I feel about the story today is different than how I felt about it when I started. In this, story and memory are synonymous.

How I'll feel about this story after I've told it to you is a mystery. Your guess is as good as mine.

You may find my speaker contrived and annoying, or self-absorbed and annoying. I have to tell you I feel these things too. And of course the speaker's contrived. And still this is a source of my anxiety.

It's hard to elaborate further on all the sources of my anxiety because I rarely have access to the full range of my anxious feelings. Is it a coincidence that I'm wearing a back brace to prevent disc damage after six intense weeks trying to tell you this?

I have to tell you I spend a lot of time wondering if I'm telling you the truth.

I have to tell you not much changes between the beginning and the end. But I have to finish telling this story before I'm forty; otherwise, I'm the person who moved into their parents' basement and never left.

I can tell you a few basics, OK? This is the story of houses bought and sold, separation, illness, and death. Plus, you know, childhood.

The best advice I ever received was this: If a story has a beginning, it also has an end.

This advice was designed, I realize, to help me keep going, as I had already begun. And it did help. Another piece of useful advice: If you're in the dark wood, just stay there. This, in response to my: I'm in the dark wood, I'm in the dark wood, I'M IN THE DARK WOOD.

I have to tell you this is a true story. There are things I don't remember.

Affidavit

Robert Hanbridge Perham Jr., my father, was born on March 17, 1951, and died on April 30, 2014, at 2:10 p.m. of END STAGE LIVER DISEASE due to (or as a consequence of) ALCOHOLIC CIRRHOSIS.

Deposition

Bad Dead Dad: How do you know this to be true?

: This is what the death certificate says.

Bad Dead Dad: You sound surprised.

: Near the end of his life my father told me he was sick due to complications from a wisdom tooth extraction.

Bad Dead Dad: Did you believe that?

:

Bad Dead Dad: Did he believe that?

: I can't answer that question.

Bad Dead Dad: Do you want to address the term ALCOHOLIC CIRRHOSIS?

: Not right now, thank you.

Bad Dead Dad: Let's go back. Is it accurate to say that you were estranged from your father starting in 2002 until his death in 2014?

: Yes. It is, more or less, accurate.

Bad Dead Dad: As in, *to cause to be strange, or a stranger, or as a stranger (to)*?

:

Bad Dead Dad: As in, *to keep apart from experience of or acquaintance with*?

: Yes.

Bad Dead Dad: What do you mean when you say, "more or less"?

: We spoke a couple of times.
We saw each other a couple of
times.

Bad Dead Dad: How many
times?

: Three times I can remember. In
the few months before he died.

: As in, *to render alien; to regard or
treat as alien.*

Bad Dead Dad: Would you like to
add this to your statement?

: I mean, I can't swear to it.

: I wouldn't swear to it.

What It Wasn't

It wasn't like, Dad, I never want to see you again. It wasn't like I changed my number. It wasn't like, forever.

What It Was

It was like, Dad, I can't talk right now. It was like, I'm sorry. It was like, I'm late for class. It was like, I need some space. It was like, for now. It was like, because I don't want to. It was like, because I Need Some Space. It was like, because. It was like, because I've talked to my therapist about this. It was like, please stop calling. It was like, please. It was like, for a little while. It was like, I can't pick up. It was like, I can't. It was like, I'm twenty-one years old I'm not your mother. It was like, I'm not your therapist. Go to AA, get a sponsor. It was like me talking to my phone. It was like, I'm sorry. It was like, I already told you I'm sorry. I'm sorry I'm sorry I'm sorry. It was like, caller ID could not have been invented at a better time. It was like, oh my god. It was like, no I can't listen to your message I'm sorry. It was like, ohmygodyournumber. It was like, again. It was like you were alive in there. It was like you could get out. It was like, 978-985-4217, I'll remember you forever. It was like, maybe you were drunk but maybe you were crying. It was like, stop. It was like, why are you leaving me a hundred messages. It was like, please don't be crying. It was like you were going to get out. It was like any minute. It was like, my voicemail is full. It was like, my phone is unplugged. It was like, my inbox is full. It was like, you're not allowed to send me that in the mail. You're not allowed to leave that at my door. It was like there was knocking. It was like you were going to get in. It was like, I remember everything. It was like, I'm scared. It was like me saying, forever.

Justification Distancing Defensiveness Dissonance Denial

You have to remember I was a child.

There are things I don't remember.

I was told a lot of things.

I was one two three four five six and seven.

Sometimes my father would say, there's no money for your skating lesson. As far as I know, this was never true. You have to remember my father would say this when he was mad at me.

The lesson was, money buys happiness.

You have to remember we had *money* but we didn't have *that much* money *if you know what I mean*. If you asked me in elementary school, this is what I would have told you, italicized just like that.

The lesson was revealed in the form of a white Mercedes.

I had skating lessons ballet lessons gymnastics lessons. "Privilege" was a word I learned later.

It appeared as though my father cared about money more than anything. I was told this was a fault.

You have to remember I was a told a lot of things.

You have to remember I had a mother.

My mother said, your father cares about appearances more than anything. The white Mercedes was a convertible.

You have to remember my father liked to show off.

This is the way it appeared. A white Mercedes with the top down.

You have to remember my mother always gave me the money for my lesson. My father's threat was an empty one.

You have to remember things were going well for my father. You have to remember it was the '80s. You have to remember my father changed careers. He sold the cheese shop and now he was in finance.

Men came to our house with trucks and ladders. What had been a two-family would become a one-family. Men came and dug a swimming pool.

The lesson was, in-ground swimming pools are high-class and aboveground swimming pools are low-class.

You have to remember I was seven years old and I was aware of this.

The white Mercedes wasn't there and then it was, surprise.

Men removed the coal stove. My father landscaped the yard. Yellow purple yellow where before there was brown grass. Men brought in statuary. My mother chose kitchen tile one perfect pink away from cranberry. Men came and tiled. My mother chose wallpaper. Men came and wallpapered.

You have to remember everything was being renovated. This was a suburb of Boston.

You have to remember I liked to show off. I brought my new Huffy to school. I brought my new Cabbage Patch twins. I wasn't ashamed of anything.

The new wallpaper had tiny purple violets outlined in gold.

The lesson was, money and appearances.

My Cabbage Patch dolls were the best Cabbage Patch dolls my friends had ever seen. My friends were jealous and I knew it.

In my new bedroom, my new wallpaper would have tiny pink roses outlined in gold, isn't it beautiful? In my new bedroom, my new headboard would have pink pastel roses on a green background.

The yellow pigtails and the yellow dresses.

I knew it and I liked it.

You have to remember my mother was an accomplice.

Men came and admired the white Mercedes in the driveway.

The pink roses and the green backgrounds.

Men came and removed a staircase. We climbed a ladder to the second floor through the hole in the ceiling.

You have to remember when I see jonquils, I feel a lot of affection for my father.

You have to remember I thought this was a great adventure. I had a basketball hoop in front of the garage and a swing set behind the garage. You have to remember we were suburban white New England.

Yes my childhood was happy. You have to understand I say this without irony.

I climbed the ladder saying the word "renovation" quietly to myself.

You have to remember we were learning to like things.

You have to admit it's a beautiful word.

Behind the garage, my father and the men smoked weed. This is a fact my mother told me later but she used the word "grass."

You have to remember that I looked down on anyone with an above-ground swimming pool.

You have to picture my father on the swing or the rings or the monkey bars with a joint in his mouth. You have to remember my father was still a young man. You have to remember my father could be silly.

That summer we three slept on a mattress in our living room beside the hole in the floor. Then my brother arrived and it was we four. This is one of my happiest memories and I have many happy memories. Soon we would have a living room on the first floor too.

The staircase was replaced. The hole was closed.

You have to remember my father's latent alcoholism was revealed in the activity behind the garage. This is what my mother told me later and by then it made a lot of sense.

My father paid for everything.

When I think of my father smoking weed, I feel a lot of affection for him.

When I think of my mother saying "grass," I remember this was all a long time ago.

You have to remember the white Mercedes was, my father said, a gift for my mother. A surprise.

After the renovation, everyone went back to their own rooms. My parents' room was now my room; my room was now my brother's. My mother's crescent moon still turned on its fishing wire in my new window. His blue face made face shapes on my new floor.

This appeared to happen all at once.

You have to remember I was a child. There are things I don't remember. I remember I was afraid to sleep alone.

I spent a lot of nights lying on the stairs watching my mother watch *Perry Mason* on TV. I also did this before the renovation. The lesson was, some things stay the same forever.

You have to remember we were learning what money can buy.

The color coldness cleanness of the kitchen tile are three things I still miss. The *Perry Mason* music still scares me.

My father was a dry alcoholic before the renovation and an alcoholic alcoholic after the renovation. This is the story my mother and I maintain.

The new bed didn't change anything.

You have to watch me watching my mother's blue profile through the bars of the banister. You have to know I spent years looking at her face.

In this way, the lesson was revealed.

You have to remember my room was on the third floor. The men put in a window seat. On the window seat was a dollhouse. To a child a staircase divides the world in half.

I've never wanted anything as much as I wanted to be with my mother.

You have to remember the first thing my mother taught me in my new room. The lesson was how to use the fire ladder. Drag its box from the closet. Lay the ladder out long on the floor. Hang it correctly from the windowsill.

And climb down?

Yes.

Do I have to?

The indoor swing disappeared. You have to remember wicker furniture was now only acceptable outside by the pool. You have to remember my parents were changing from hippie to yuppie. You have to remember the phrase was "upwardly mobile." The white Mercedes revealed this as it also revealed my father's propensity toward mania.

You have to remember it was the Reagans.

The year my parents bought the house, they converted it from a one-family into a two-family. This is how they would pay the mortgage. This was the year of my father's depression that connected his job in the cheese shop to his job in finance, and the year my mother taught kindergarten during the day and painted walls at night. My mother paid for everything.

Soon it would be the Bushes and the Clintons.

From afar, my mother's mother diagnosed manic-depressive illness in my father. This is perhaps what they call an armchair diagnosis. This is a story my mother told me later. You have to remember it made a lot of sense.

The depression and rage that preceded or followed the episode, I don't remember, just the white Mercedes in the driveway. It wasn't a great surprise. You have to remember we were used to my father's spending sprees.

You have to remember my father could be the life of the party.

I liked to say the phrase "spending spree" quietly to myself.

My mother's mother was a psychologist. We all thought she was crazy and in this we were united.

You have to remember my father liked to have a good time. My father was a great host. You have to remember that after the renovation we had a basement with a refrigerator full of soda and a freezer full of things you'd find on an ice cream truck.

You have to remember we were used to the depression that followed each spending spree, when I would sometimes spend the week with my aunt, whom I loved second only to my mother. And at bedtime I still wanted my mother.

You have to remember the fire ladder was heavy. It was hard to drag the box out of the closet.

You have to remember we were used to the rage that followed each spending spree, when my mother would send me upstairs and block the stairs with her body.

You have to remember I know a thing or two about self-medicating.

I spent a lot of time imagining the fire ladder in its box in the closet.

I'm still a poor sleeper.

After the renovation my mother floated my brother around me in the pool. My friends spent most weekends at our house. My father drove the white Mercedes to work all summer. The ice cream truck visited our street regularly.

My favorite game was playing therapist to my dolls.

You have to remember that children of alcoholics have a certain amount in common.

You have to remember my mother said, if you see fire, you do not come down the stairs.

Here's the first story I knew about my father: Soon after you were born, he came home from work, picked you up, and dropped you on your head.

I've known this story for as long as I can remember and I can only tell it like that, in my mother's voice.

You have to remember there are certain patterns.

After the renovation, my father was either coming home from work and cannonballing into the pool, or he was crying at the brand-new kitchen counter.

The phrase "dropped you on your head" seemed funny to me from the beginning.

He had a drink in his hand either way but I think that goes without saying.

One doll was always the bad doll. I took detailed notes enumerating the ways she was bad. I always came to the conclusion that I couldn't help her. Come back next week.

Yes I'm aware of *The Drama of the Gifted Child* but I wasn't then.

You have to remember the crying was scary whereas the yelling was not.

The phrase "dropped you on your head" sounds like a punchline.

You have to remember the fire ladder was all metal rungs connected by chain long enough to reach three stories down to the driveway. You have to remember I practiced dragging it and hanging it and looking down at the driveway.

You have to remember I had a mother who felt a lot of things.

After the head-dropping incident, my mother kicked my father out. He was back a few days later promising never to drink again.

You have to remember my mother did not believe for a second that the white Mercedes was for her.

Even with a freezer full of ice cream I wanted ice cream from the ice cream truck.

You have to remember my parents stayed together until I went to college. You have to remember the divorce went on for years and these years have long since become one year. Of the memory of this long year I can only say, we never recovered.

You have to remember my mother would usually call me down from the stairs to sleep in her lap. These nights have long since become one night and the memory of this night is among my happiest memories.

Remember Rocket Firecracker Chipwich Creamsicle? Remember all of them advertised in full-color pictures? Remember when you heard the music and the bells you could see these pictures in your mind?

My mother told me, that car is not a gift.

I imagined landing safely on the hood of the white Mercedes while the house burned down.

You have to remember I was already my mother's best friend.

You have to remember the one doll never recovered but the others were happy. In this way the play could continue.

You have to remember my mother was also a first-rate yeller. You have to remember I always believed she was stronger than my father.

If you see fire, you do not come down the stairs.

And thus I was safe.

After the head-dropping incident my father didn't drink again until after the renovation. When I think of my father not drinking for seven years, I feel great affection for him.

When I think of my mother not giving up her position on the stairs.

When I heard the music and the bells in the street I said, please please please please.

You have to remember I saw my mother cry exactly once during my childhood and this she did in the closet with the fire ladder. That this is one of my most terrifying memories I think goes without saying.

As soon as you hear the bells and sirens it seems as though the bells and sirens are driving away.

Remember how hot a driveway can get in the summer? Remember blacktop? You have to picture the make-believe town my mother drew in chalk disappearing in the drips from our bathing suits.

You have to believe those seven years were a gift and my father gave that gift to me. You have to remember it's hard to talk yourself out of the things you want.

Please please please please.

My mother always gave me the money.

Did I say I loved the white Mercedes? Picture me sitting in the jump seat and my father driving fast down Route 1. When I say this is a happy memory, the memory begins to vibrate as though it will break.

My mother showed me how to fry an egg on the blacktop. I was a child: There are things I remember. I ran out to the street barefoot. The popsicle dripped red and blue. Pool water only protects you so long on tar.

Sometimes my mother is still the only person who can comfort me. It's easy to blame my father for a lot of things and it's easy to feel great affection for him.

My mother rechalked the town. The lesson is, some things stay the same forever.

At night I watched my brother sleeping in the crib. I imagined lifting him and climbing down the ladder one-handed when the time came.

You have to remember how easy it is to weight the facts any way you want.

Yes I practiced.

The house never burned down.

Another Day in Paradise

My father checkerboards the lawn with the mower, first up then across. Wonderland! is what I think, but this is Vermont. Later we sit on the deck and my father offers me the yellow of his hard-boiled egg, which I don't like. We try to remember some stories from when we were little but I can't come up with much. Because I'm twelve, there isn't much. Either that, or there's everything.

When I was twelve, my father says, there was football in the street, mowing the lawn, my dad's heart attack in the white chair in the living room in the middle of the day.

The chair is still in Nana's living room, next to the television.

Good Dad-in-the-Sky: Yes, this is all true.

There wasn't time for an ambulance, to take off his glasses.

My father takes off his glasses and lies back on his lawn chair. Out there's the one living apple tree in an orchard of dead ones. It's the only one that's green. All the rest are yellow. My father has resurrected it. Every weekend he's out there in my grandfather's orchard.

Bad Dead Dad: Your mother was the one who told you about the white chair.

See how green.

At dusk when it's cool, my father drags the hose across the lawn between the delphinium and bleeding heart, which is our favorite plant no kidding, and through the break in the wall. In the orchard, he's making a ritual circle around the tree: Miracle-Gro and water. I follow him to the wall but don't wade into the tall grass because I'm afraid of getting ticks on my legs.

What a day! he calls as he sprays. We're getting apples! I sit down in the grass, which is lawn, on my side of the wall.

When he's finished, he coils the hose under the edge of the deck and stretches back out on his chair. His feet twist like the branches of that tree and that's what I tell him. Will my feet look like that when I'm old? My father shakes his head.

Bad Dead Dad and Good Dad-in-the-Sky shake their dad heads.

Bad Dead Dad: Now you're making everything up.

I made up the hardboiled egg at the beginning because it seemed like we should be sharing something at the beginning.

Bad Dead Dad: I told you so.

I made up the part where my father tells me about his father because it seemed like he should be the one to tell me. I made up the part where my father tells me about the ambulance and the glasses. It's my mother who tells me this story and I never speak of it with my father.

Good Dad-in-the-Sky: It's OK, we expected this.

The bleeding heart's for real, no kidding.

Bad Dead Dad: Maudlin.

When I have questions, I ask my mother.

My father's looking out at the apple tree. It looks like heaven out there, he says.

Good Dad-in-the-Sky: It is. When you close your eyes, it all disappears.

Another day in paradise, my father says, closing his eyes.

Are We Having Fun Yet?

The Dead Dads come with me everywhere, even to the funeral home. Here they are in the parking lot, leaning against my brother's truck. Sometimes I want to be alone so I work on banishing them. You'd think it would be easy since I made them up, but it isn't. What a day, Good Dad-in-the-Sky says. It's the prettiest day.

Let's do this, my brother says like we're superheroes about to go in guns blazing. We're on the wide white porch of the Eustis & Cornell Funeral Home. We're ringing the Eustis & Cornell Funeral Home bell.

I'll see you later, I say to the Dead Dads. But the Dead Dads don't go away. They are the two pillars behind me.

Stay here, I say. I want to make the decisions without you. It doesn't bother us, Good Dad-in-the-Sky says. We're with you.

The door opens and we go inside. Bad Dead Dad is working hard to get up the last step. I can feel him almost not breathing.

My brother and I sit on a floral couch. The Eustis & Cornell Funeral Home Funeral Director says something something and then he slides some papers across the polished table. Sign sign sign initial. Good Dad-in-the-Sky unwraps a complimentary Eustis & Cornell peppermint from the crystal bowl.

Are we having fun yet? he says.

One clarification, Funeral Director says, for the death certificate. Was your father Robert Hanbridge Perham the Third or Robert Hanbridge Perham Junior?

My brother and I look at each other.

Our father was . . . ?

Our father used to say, are we having fun yet? I tell Funeral Director's reflection in the polished table.

Our father was.

Robert Hanbridge Perham the Third or Robert Hanbridge Perham Junior?

He said it when we really were having fun. Like when we were in a swimming pool.

The brochures on the table fan out saying, *A Dignity Memorial Provider, A Dignity Memorial . . . , A Dignity . . . , A Dig . . .*

My brother goes outside to bring in my mother.

Nice, Bad Dead Dad says. Good for you two. You don't even know your father's name.

Bad Dead Dad is breathing hard, holding on to the Eustis & Cornell Funeral Home's funereal front window treatments. I wait to see a cloud of dust rise around his head but there isn't one. I imagine Funeral Director with his colorless hair standing on one of the floral chairs, vacuuming the drapes with a brush attachment. Oh the indignity, Good Dad-in-the-Sky says and unwraps another peppermint.

My brother sits down on the floral couch. My mother sits down on the floral couch. She thinks it's Robert Hanbridge Perham the Third.

"Indignity" is not one of my father's words so it must be mine.

How do you not know for sure? I say.

I haven't thought about your father in years, she says.

My brother takes a complimentary Eustis & Cornell pen from the jar and spins it through his fingers.

I think it's Junior, I say, but I think Mom's right.

Well, which is it? my brother says. He looks at me like, no way I'm deciding this.

I don't know, I say. Funeral Director says not to worry. We can tell him the answer when we come back later today.

We can't come back later today, my mother says. Then she goes back out into the parking lot.

Will you pay the deposit in cash? Check?

Yes?

Pay to the order of: <u>The Eustis & Cornell Funeral Home</u>

Funeral Director goes upstairs to write the receipt.

Four-thousand-dollar mint? my brother says. Thank god we almost laugh.

Don't mind if I do, buddy, Good Dad-in-the-Sky says and unwraps another. The candy cracks in his teeth.

We're taking all these mints, I say, and the pens.

Put 'em in your purse, my brother says.

Bad Dead Dad is over by the decorative fireplace picking up the sample urns one by one.

◆

I want to be alone talking to Lawyer so I work on banishing the Dead Dads. You'd think it would be easy since I made them up, but it isn't. They are the pair of leather chairs behind me. Stay out here in reception, I say.

What are we going to do, ride the elevator up and down? Good Dad-in-the-Sky says. Honey, we've got a better elevator than this, let me tell you.

A Heavenelevator? I say. Good one, Good Dad-in-the-Sky says.

For a minute I almost believe in the Dead Dads and the Heavenelevator.

My brother's wife and son are riding the actual elevator up and down. Every few minutes the doors open and there they are. Dada!

the baby says, his hands in the air like ta-da! Then the doors close. Are we having fun yet? Good Dad-in-the-Sky says.

My brother and my mother prowl around in front of the reception desk.

That's not going to last long, my brother says about the baby entertained by the elevator, so we better hurry it up.

Bad Dead Dad maneuvers into one of the leather chairs. His eyes disappear into his face disappears into his neck disappears into his jacket, which he's zipped all the way up. Cold in here, he says. Get me a cup of tea.

The last time I saw my father alive he was in a hospital and this was months ago. He said, get me a cup of tea. A nurse said, no dear, not right now. My father said, Brittany, get me a cup of tea, and I said, in a little while, Dad, and it had been a long time since I'd called anyone Dad.

No dear, not right now.

Now it's our turn in the conference room. We sit in high-backed Lawyer chairs around a shining Lawyer table.

Since when did my father drink tea? Coffee, black.

This is where you've brought me, Bad Dead Dad says standing at the window. Half a question mark. Outside is the office park and the highway leading into Boston, which is already getting trafficky.

If we don't leave soon, we're going to be in that, my mother says.

It's the prettiest day, even over the parking lot. The sun shines in around Bad Dead Dad's head.

I remember your father, Lawyer says getting his Lawyer pen ready. This Lawyer is the last of my mother's divorce lawyers and the only lawyer I know in the state of Massachusetts.

This is going to be juicy, Good Dad-in-the-Sky says and spins around in his chair. For a minute his legs twirl straight out off the ground like he's a little boy.

Lawyer is shuffling through the heap of paper my brother's dumped from a cardboard box. In there's the will.

Is it the last will? Lawyer wants to know.

It's what we could find in his house in twenty minutes this morning, my brother says. He breaks the box down with his foot.

OK. OK . . . OK, your father made you the executor of his estate, Lawyer says to my brother. OK?

My practical well-equipped calm adult little brother.

OK, my brother says.

You're in real trouble, Bad Dead Dad says. Now he's wearing a wool suit even though it's April. He's standing up straighter, smoothing down his hair, which is looking darker. He's getting younger, charming. He clasps his hands behind his back and even though I can't see, I know he's wearing his gold rings and cuff links. He squints over the field of my father's papers. This is something he understands. The helixes on his tie are silverfish. Lawyer's pen clicks.

◆

I don't want to be alone in my father's house, and for a minute, at my father's door, the Dead Dads hesitate. Aren't you coming in? I say. Good Dad-in-the-Sky is the mailbox and Bad Dead Dad is the door knocker. Stop that, I say. This isn't *A Christmas Carol*. So we all go inside.

I walk all around and look at everything until there aren't any more closed doors. There are some scary things I'm not ready to mention.

We're standing in my father's closet. The door of my father's safe has been cut off its hinges but I'm not ready to think about that.

Where are all my father's suits? I say. There are a few Champion sweatshirts on the hangers and a few pairs of wind pants. There's an undershirt that used to be white. This isn't my father's closet.

It is, Bad Dead Dad says.

My father didn't wear undershirts. He wore starched white dress shirts with nothing underneath. He wore cuff links, brass and monogrammed or porcelain shaped like the hot and cold taps on a bathroom sink or gold-plated, his father's. He wore suits, double-breasted with gold buttons or pinstriped or charcoal, wool that picked up the smell of the cold. He wore a black belt with a gold buckle. He wore ties with paisley with DNA helixes with Botticelli's Venus, ties I bought for Father's Days floating up out of tissue and tie boxes, never a surprise, on doorknobs and over the posts of my parents' bed or untied around his neck coming home on a day like today, sweating, his shirtsleeves rolled up. I remember the ties and the suits and the buckle and the belt and the cuff links and the father coming home exactly.

That was a long time ago, Good Dad-in-the-Sky says.

That was a pretty description, Bad Dead Dad says. Could be anyone's father.

Are we having fun yet? I say to hold my father's expression in my mouth. Then I feel like I'm going to cry. Bad Dead Dad is standing in the middle of the closet with his fists in his eyes.

I want to fold the undershirt but I'm afraid to touch it.

Good Dad-in-the-Sky steers me out of the closet with his hands on my shoulders. Let's go out to the garage and find your mother, he says.

Instead, I go down the hall to a spare bedroom with a sheetless bed and a closet door accordioned open. A box of new wineglasses on the shelf, paper napkins, a shape in a garbage bag. I lie down on the floor. Underneath the nightstand is a blue glass half-moon with its face against the wall. I know this moonman because he hung in the window of my childhood bedroom. I pull him out and hold his sharp point against my stomach. Moonman looks at me with his man's nose and one closed eye and where are the Dead Dads?

Dust, dust. I scrape it from his blue face with my finger.

I wish Good Dad-in-the-Sky would come in here and tell me the story of how the moonman got beneath the nightstand until my mother comes in and turns on the light.

It's your moon, she says. I can fix it, it's just missing a hook. Let's go downstairs and find your brother. She dusts the moonman on her jeans.

I follow her down into the kitchen. She wraps the moonman in newspaper and puts it in the box of Things We're Taking, which she carries out to her car.

What would my father say if he knew I let my mother in his house?

Good Dad-in-the-Sky is leaning on the kitchen counter drinking a Diet Coke, shirtsleeves up. Bad Dead Dad is in the dining room inspecting my father's father's Purple Heart, which is framed above the table. You're going to throw this away, he says.

I'm hungry, Good Dad-in-the-Sky says. Bad Dead Dad says, I'd settle for a drink.

In my father's kitchen there are double ovens, stainless steel burners, pans hanging above a marble island, blocks of knives, jars of spatulas and tongs, and this drawer of prescriptions, OxyContin 10 mg 20 mg 40 mg. Were you expecting silverware? Bad Dead Dad says. A mostly empty refrigerator, nothing to rot.

My father was a wonderful cook but I don't know what he knows (knew).

A sliding door, a deck, a day moon eyes the garden.

Deposition

Bad Dead Dad: Let's try this again.

:

Bad Dead Dad: Start at the beginning.

: What's the beginning?

Good Dad-in-the-Sky: A death, or a birth.

Affidavit

Robert Hanbridge Perham Jr. died in the ICU of Massachusetts General Hospital on April 30, 2014, at 2:10 p.m. He was born in Malden, Massachusetts, on March 17, 1951. He was called Bobby or Bobby Jr. by his mother. He went to work in a greenhouse after his father died. His mother went to work as a secretary and lined the edges of her stairs with canned goods. He attended Reading High School. He blew out his knee playing JV baseball. He married Leigh Wellington, who also attended Reading High School, on September 14, 1973. She called him Bob. She finished college. They turned twenty-three. She went to graduate school. He worked in a cheese factory. She opened a preschool. He opened a cheese store. She named the store the Continental Cow. They spent each Christmas season packing gift boxes. She added a kindergarten. His cheese logs coated in pistachios were legendary. They went to Greece. They bought a house. He sold the store. He went to work as an insurance salesman. She added an elementary school. They turned thirty. They had a daughter. He stopped drinking. He opened his own office. They renovated their house. They added a swimming pool. They had a son. The children had birthdays they recorded on VHS tapes. They sent Christmas cards. They turned forty. They were seldom alone together. He stayed downstairs and she stayed upstairs with the children, who were home from swimming lessons, skating lessons, violin lessons. The children were in school plays. The word "alcoholic" entered the family language. It was a word he never said. They disliked being alone together. They went to Italy, France, and Germany with the children. They celebrated their twentieth anniversary with a big party. The son played T-ball then Little League. The daughter went to college. They were never alone together. They lived on separate floors of the house. He cashed out their savings. They separated. He liquidated her 401(k). They turned fifty. They hired lawyers. He bought a house in a neighboring suburb. She went to his office in the middle of the night and discovered he'd cashed out their savings and liquidated her 401(k). The son lived with her and visited him on weekends. She borrowed money. She hired a forensic lawyer. The son had an asthma attack at school and was admitted to the pediatric ICU in Massachusetts General Hospital. They went to arbitration. The son was intubated. She went to the courthouse to apply for a restraining order. He fired his lawyer. She was told by the judge not to file the restraining order: It usually makes things worse. The son was extubated. The son was released and readmitted. The son was tested for allergies. The tests came back negative. She looked for other triggers. She had the fertilizer on the baseball field tested. She had the paint on the football field tested. She was told by the attending, two triggers make things worse. The son was released and readmitted. She couldn't pay the mortgage. They went to court. They never found a cause. They saw a judge. She sold him her half of the house for $1. The son was released and readmitted and released. She couldn't pay rent. She moved with the son to her parents' house in Vermont where she lives today. The son started high school. She signed the papers. He signed the papers. They were divorced. The order cites "irreconcilable differences." He remarried. He acquired a stepson and a stepdaughter, both grown. His new wife died of an unspecified illness. He never stopped drinking. He bought a house in another suburb. The son recovered and lives in Vermont with his children today. The daughter moved to California where she lives today. He got a new girlfriend. His new girlfriend became his ex-girlfriend. He was found somnolent in his home by a visiting nurse. He never regained consciousness. He died in the ICU in Massachusetts General Hospital forty-four days after his sixty-third birthday on April 30, 2014, at 2:10 p.m. of END STAGE LIVER DISEASE due to (or as a consequence of) ALCOHOLIC CIRRHOSIS.

Deposition

Bad Dead Dad: Swear to it?

:

Lock and Key

The father is out there with a key that doesn't fit this lock. We're in here with a baseball bat. The father in the story has parked his car in the driveway that isn't his driveway. Not anymore. The father and mother have been separated all year. The father is yelling something out there in the street. The mother in the story won't be home until Monday. The mother doesn't believe in shades or sheers or blinds or curtains so all the windows up here are bare to the sky and yelling. We don't believe in windows so we're lying on the floor. The neighbor in the story is draping his arm over the fence that separates the yards. The neighbor is offering the father a beer. The beer in the story is Bud and in the father's hand. Up here we can hear everything.

Up here we can hear everything. We have all the pillows off the couch and in front of the TV. One of us is home from college and one of us is home from the hospital. We have a bedsheet and sitcoms all night. We believe in *TGIF* and in keeping the sheet over us even when it's sticky hot. The mother in the story doesn't believe in AC. When it's light and we're brave and it's so hot we can't stand it we leave each second-floor window open one crack for air and listening. This never applies to first-floor windows. We have it all set up. We have pillows and a sheet and more food than we can reasonably eat. We don't believe in the first floor after dark and it's getting dark.

We don't believe in the first floor after dark and it's getting dark. My brother doesn't believe in the first floor ever. When it's earlier and I'm braver I go down to make mac and cheese and frozen peas while he watches the street. No father, he yells down. We believe in voice contact. The mother leaves us money for delivery but we don't believe in doorbells or feet on the front steps. We believe in Ring Dings and Cheetos and Fruit Roll-Ups. The kitchen door in the story is glass and big as an ice rink. The kitchen door is the one that bothers me. I set the houseplants out like landmines. No father, he yells. I believe in early warning systems. I turn on the lights and check the locks even though I don't believe locks are going to do one damn thing. Mac and cheese and peas and Ring Dings and Cheetos and Fruit Roll-Ups and Cokes on a cookie sheet. And Pop-Tarts. Father, he yells and I go upstairs. The kitchen in the story is now off-limits.

The kitchen in the story is now off-limits. The kitchen is all lit up. Also the hallway and the dining room and the bathroom. We believe in lights twenty-four hours. The house in the story is big and bright and anyone can see right through it. The father in the story is yelling something out there in the street. We don't believe in standing up so we can't see the driveway, the father, or the neighbor reaching over the fence that separates the yards. We can hear everything but we refuse to hear exact words. The neighbor is cracking a joke. My brother unwraps a Fruit Roll-Up. Prednisone, Fruit Roll-Up. The prednisone in the story makes my brother eat constantly. I say, eat your peas. But I don't believe he has to eat peas if he doesn't want to and he knows it. The neighbor is cracking a beer. My brother unwraps a Fruit Roll-Up. Fruit Roll-Up, nebulizer. He slips the face mask over his mouth. Up here we have a tight schedule.

Up here we have a tight schedule. Because I'm the grown-up in this story it's my job to keep it. Because he's not sure how grown-up I am, it's my brother's job to do what I say. The nebulizer sits between us on the pillow. The nebulizer is our kitten, our puppy. It's going to be loud, he says into the face mask. We don't believe in loud. It's fine, I say. I crack the albuterol vial and fill the reservoir. He crosses the baseball bat over his chest. I connect reservoir to face mask. We don't believe the bat is going to do one damn thing. He adjusts the elastic strap around his head. I hit the switch. The nebulizer purrs and the face mask fogs. He breathes and breathes and breathes and breathes and breathes. *Step by Step* and *TGIF* is almost done. I tap the reservoir with my finger. Almost gone. I believe in every last drop.

I believe in every last drop. I believe in nebulizers more than I believe in quiet, more than I believe in lights or locks or bats or being scared. I believe in keeping us out of the ER. I believe in parking my car on the street just in case. The driveway is off-limits. The father in the story is yelling something in the street and it's dark out there. I believe in our television. I believe in the sound the back gate makes when the father opens it. The gate sound is an early warning system. I believe the father is following the blacktop down behind the house. I believe in the moment of panic after our shows end and before the news begins, and I believe in the sound the garage door makes when the father opens it. The garage door sound is an early warning system. I believe in the ten o'clock news, and in the eleven o'clock news, and that the Disney Channel can be counted on all night. I believe the father is in the dark behind the house. I believe in the creak of the stairs leading to the back porch. The creak is an early warning system. I know the difference between a wheeze and a sneeze and a cough and a snore and phlegm in the back of the throat. I believe the breath will tell me everything I need to know. I will hear whatever it is on the back porch. I will hear it before it reaches the kitchen door. If things go wrong, I believe in calling the nurse's line and if I have to, I believe in paging the on-call doctor at five-minute intervals until he calls me back. I believe nothing on the Disney Channel will be upsetting. I am the mother and I stay up all night. I will hear whatever it is on the back porch. I will hear it. I believe I can hear the alveoli vibrate way down in the chest. The breath is an early warning system. I believe the father is at the kitchen door. I believe in pounding on the chest. I believe the breath is fog on glass. I will count on it all night. I believe the father is looking into our house. I believe the father is crying. The father is out there with a key that doesn't fit this lock. The father is leaning toward us and the story tells me everything I need to know.

Jonquils

Friday, my mother says.

The weekend would be fine, I say.

My father's ex-girlfriend-now-friend looks skeptical. That's soon, she says.

We're all on the enclosed back porch of the Eustis & Cornell Funeral Home. My father's ex-girlfriend-now-friend hasn't decided if she's coming in or if she isn't. She's bracing the screen door open on one nyloned calf.

How will we reach all his friends before the weekend? she says. Bob had lots of friends.

A dry-cleaning bag is shimmying against her. She's trying to keep it under control, holding the hanger in one hand and the plastic tail in the other. She's brought my father a black suit to be burned in.

I went by the house, she says, on my way here.

Between prepositional phrases, my father's closet opens with a breath of wool and snow.

She's wearing a black suit and her blond hair doesn't move an inch.

Do you have to wear a suit to be cremated? I want everyone to know right now that I'll be going naked into the fire but I keep my mouth shut.

Funeral Director says he has another event taking place in the front of the house at this hour; he's terribly sorry he's had to greet us here in back. He's already told us, so now he's telling her.

We stand around looking mournful on the indoor-outdoor carpet. Except my mother who's looking bored. She twirls the cord for the blinds around her thumb. In the parking lot, my brother's baby is standing in the driver's seat of the car yelling vroom vroom. My brother's wife sits with the passenger door open, a sandal hanging off her big toe. In here we have folded-up folding chairs, cardboard boxes with curling flaps, an upright piano under a quilt, and nowhere to sit down. This place is too crowded for the Dead Dads.

It's good to see you, my father's ex-girlfriend-now-friend says and decides to come in and hug my brother. The screen door thwacks closed. My mother lets go of the cord and the blinds zip down a few inches before she catches it.

It's good to see you too, Brittany, my father's ex-girlfriend-now-friend says. Quick hug. I've met her before but somehow I can't remember it.

◆

Where were we when I met her? I grill my brother on this point as we drive up and down Route 128 doing after-death errands. Windows open, hair in my mouth, the baby in the car seat yelling no no no don't want cracker!

Do I look like I remember? my brother says retracting the cracker and charging through lanes of traffic. I've seen her a shit-ton lately.

Well I can't remember, I say. Can you please drive like a normal person.

Massholes can't drive, I'll tell you that for free, my brother says because he lives in Vermont now.

We're going to die, I say.

Fact, he says.

We're going to be late for Eustis & Cornell, I say.

She's a clone of the second wife, he says. You don't remember her because you aren't here.

Can we roll up some windows?

You want my kid to throw a shit-fit? The wind's the only thing keeping him under control back there.

My brother tries again with the cracker, reaching it back between the front seats until the baby smacks it out of his hand, no no Daddy don't want that want ice cream!

We're getting you ice cream if you're a good boy, my brother yells. Jesus fucking, why did you tell him we're getting ice cream?

Obviously I have no idea what I'm doing, I say.

He brakes behind the fender of a semi. Rush hour.

Ice cream you said you said Dad-dy you said, the baby wails.

I know buddy, my brother says. Dad's three blonds. Mom divorced, Wife Two dead, and now, ladies and gentlemen, we have a survivor.

◆

The survivor hands me the bag with my father's suit inside. I hold the hanger on one finger until it goes numb and then I transfer it to a second finger. She touches my arm. I'm sorry this isn't under better circumstances, she says.

I see I'm prepared to make her the villain in this whole thing. My mother hoists the blinds to the top of the window frame and fiddles with the cord. What the hell, she says, this thing's broken.

I take the cord and stir it around until the blinds lock in place.

Why not Friday? my mother says.

Friday is quite soon, Funeral Director says, quite soon. All your husband's loved ones might not be able . . .

Funeral Director looks back and forth: my mother, my father's ex-girlfriend-now-friend. The baby amps up his vrooming in the parking lot and Funeral Director looks like he might run.

You have to fly home, my mother says to me, because you live in California. So let's just do it already.

She's right, I say meaning my father's ex-girlfriend-now-friend. Is Saturday possible?

My father had a lot of friends.

We generally don't advise arranging an event on such short notice, Funeral Director says, but I believe we can accommodate you if that's what you decide you want. Let me just take a quick look.

He disappears into the Eustis & Cornell Funeral Home. When the door opens, we hear a few notes of piped-in funeral music.

Is that the Beatles on the effing harpsichord? my brother says politely. We're not going with that, I'll tell you that for free.

I crush my free hand between two folding chairs so I don't laugh. Nothing but the vrooming outside and my mother whooshing the blinds up and down until Funeral Director comes back. Yes, indeed, he can accommodate our party on Saturday at one p.m.

Would you like me to arrange for a chaplain? he says. There's a nice man we frequently work with who—

No, my mother says.

Yes, my father's ex-girlfriend-now-friend says.

—might be available on short notice, Funeral Director finishes.

We look at each other. My brother looks at me like, no way I'm deciding this.

What's a minister going to do? my mother says. He wasn't religious. We don't want a religious service for Christ's sake.

I see I'm prepared to make her the villain in this whole thing.

What will we do without a chaplain? my father's ex-girlfriend-now-friend says. What will people do when they come?

I recommend a chaplain, Funeral Director says. He'll deliver a few words. It will provide a . . . structure. I can ask him to keep things . . . nondenominational. It's quite . . . comforting to everyone.

We'll take the chaplain, I say.

Of course, he says, we won't be able to have the cremains with us on such short notice. It will be at least a week until the crematorium we work with will be able to . . . prepare . . .

It's fine, my brother says. My father's ex-girlfriend-now-friend braces herself against the upright piano.

I'm so sorry for you two, she says.

I'm thinking about cremains and the Lydia Davis story about cremains and considering all the things my complaint letter to the Eustis & Cornell Funeral Home will say when I write it. I let my hanger finger go completely numb.

Of course, Funeral Director says, we will provide a temporary urn in the absence of the cremains so people will have a place to pay their respects. Perhaps you can provide a picture of your father that we might place beside the urn, with the flowers . . . a small altar?

Bob had headshots taken for his business cards, my father's ex-girlfriend-now-friend says. Some time ago. He looks so handsome. There's an 8 × 10 in the living room. I'll pick it up when I go back over.

That will be perfect, Funeral Director says. Perfect.

My father's ex-girlfriend-now-friend reaches over and grips my free fingers. There was nothing in your father's safe, she says.

I'm ready to cede my father's house and my father's funeral and my father's flowers and my father's headshot and my father's ashes and my father's remaining suits and whatever it was in my father's safe over to her. The survivor.

As for the flowers, Funeral Director says, or if there are any other personal touches you'd like to have, we can suggest . . .

We'll take care of the flowers, I say. Jonquils.

My father's ex-girlfriend-now-friend looks skeptical. Jonquils, she says sadly.

OK, my mother says. Great. She's holding the screen door open and picking at the hole in her jeans. Her blond hair stands straight up in the wind. Behind her is a hill leading up into the suburban woods. There are a few yellow flowers but from here I can't tell if they're dandelions, which my father hated, or the starts of jonquils. The jonquils are coming in everywhere all over town and unless someone's ripped them up, they'll be coming in along the borders of our old backyard where my father planted them.

I'll take that, Funeral Director says. I swing the hanger off my finger and hand it over. What a lovely suit.

My Finest Moment

Lawyer says, good evening. It turns out, your father made you his executrix instead of your brother.

How could this happen!

Legally, your father made you his executrix shortly before he passed away. This happens. I'm looking at the paperwork. It's certified. Shortly before some-one passes away, they often change the will. There was a lot of paperwork but he's certified this addendum. So that's the end of it.

Even if he changed the will, why would he make this addendum! That's not the end of it! He knew my brother better! Why would he pick me when he knew my brother better! It doesn't make sense to pick me! He lived in Massachusetts! It doesn't make

sense geographically! It's a night-
mare! I live in California!

Well, your father had a reason—

Geographically it's a nightmare! I'll have to fly back and forth all the time!

Well. Your father had a reason. It turns out he wanted you for his executrix. And you won't have to fly back and forth all the time. Good evening, Lawyer says.

Some Truths About Housing Markets

I'm trying to sell my father's house because he's dead and I'm the executrix and it's my job. I'm trying to figure out some things about housing markets because I've never bought or sold a house before. I'm also trying to figure out some things about my father. Good Dad-in-the-Sky and Bad Dead Dad aren't any help. Because I've made them up, they know what I know. Both of them are shaking their heads like, good luck, sweetheart.

The house I'm selling, my father's house, where he lived for the last ten years of his life, is in Marblehead, Massachusetts. Marblehead is an expensive and desirable suburb of Boston. I know this from growing up, because this is where, my father said, the rich people lived, and from the Realtor, who says so.

My father, now that he's dead, owes a lot of people a lot of money.

My mother wants to know where all the money went. What did he do with her retirement? What did he do with her savings? Why was he mortgaged to the hilt? she says. He was a goddamn financial planner. Your father sold our house—your growing-up house!—in Beverly for $825,000! she says. Where's all that money?

I investigate. Trulia.com says our house sells for $625,000 on 7/23/2003, in a "Purchase/Resale Arm's-Length Residential Transaction." 2003 is the year my father sells our house to some other family.

You don't know anything about this, Bad Dead Dad says. So just stop it.

Trulia.com also registers a previous sale of our house in Beverly on 7/7/2003 in a "Non-Arm's-Length Transaction," which must be the day my mother sells her half of our house to my father. Selling price: $1. I know this type of sale happens frequently in the real-estate business, but I don't understand the mechanics.

$625,000, I say to my mother.

Still, my mother says.

Our house in Beverly is built in 1890 as the summer home of President Benjamin Harrison. This is what I'm told, though I can find no evidence of it. If it were true, this would be a selling feature I'm sure. My parents buy our house in 1980 for $60,000, my mother remembers, and eventually my father sells it to some other family. This is the way real estate works.

My mother is notoriously bad at math.

You're notoriously bad at math too, Bad Dead Dad says.

Compared to Marblehead, Beverly is a less-expensive and less-desirable suburb of Boston, though it is still expensive and desirable: Just look at the real-estate market. And some parts of Beverly are even more expensive and even more desirable, for example, Beverly Farms. In Beverly Farms, the houses are always behind some gate and over some hill. They have carriage houses and private beaches and deep-water docks. Every room has an ocean view, picture that. This is what my father says every time we drive through, which we do frequently. Our house is in regular Beverly, not in Beverly Farms, but it has a backyard and a freestanding garage and it's a short walk to the public beaches and to the main street, which is called Main Street, and this is where I live until I go to college, and this is where home is, even after that, even now, even though some other family lives there.

I loved that house, says my mother.

In 2003, three years into my parents' separation and a year before their divorce is final, my mother moves into her parents' house in Vermont. She can't afford the mortgage on our house—where's all the money?—whereas my father has bought a condo in Swampscott with a deck that overlooks the ocean. At the end of the ocean is the whole Boston skyline. Swampscott is also an expensive and desirable suburb of Boston, though not as expensive and desirable as Marblehead. If I had to, I would say it goes something like this: Marblehead, Swampscott, Beverly.

Bad Dead Dad: Your father was moving up in the world.

I always wanted to live in Swampscott, my mother says. And he knew it.

I'm in my father's condo in Swampscott only once in the daytime. We've both just moved out of our house. I went back to college and he went to this condo by way of the Extended Stay America. A skyline view is a special feature, maybe the feature that makes my father choose the condo. I stand on the deck while my father says, look at that skyline, what a view! His wide-open arms are the horizon between blue ocean and blue sky.

I have no memories in the Marblehead house. The Marblehead house is only a house I need to sell, fast.

Because my mother can't pay the mortgage on our house in Beverly, she agrees to sell her half of it to my father for $1. In return, my father agrees to put money in an account that will send my brother to two years of college. My mother and father agree on this one thing: I will be the custodian, which means that I will manage the money on my brother's behalf until he grows up. Then my father hires people to fix the things that need fixing and sells our house to some other family for $625,000: a good profit. This is the way divorces work.

I'm pretty sure of all these things.

I love our backyard, Good Dad-in-the-Sky says. It looks just the same as it did except our flowers were better.

My father is notoriously good at making a profit and at growing flowers, especially jonquils.

My mother wants to know where all the money went: Your father couldn't have drunk it all!

Bad Dead Dad: Where are you going with all of this?

I'm in my father's condo in Swampscott only once in the nighttime. My brother has called me here and I'm not admiring the view. When there's no moon, it's hard to see what's down there beneath the deck. Beach or ocean? Can we get down there? What about at low tide?

How long is it safe to consider this question?

Bad Dead Dad: Good luck, sweetheart.

I have a lot of questions about money and a lot of questions about other things. I start by concocting a few scenarios. Were you a secret gambler? I ask the Dead Dads. Were you in debt to the mob? You couldn't have drunk it all!

It's nighttime in the condo in Swampscott and my brother has called me: Come get me. My mother drives with me from Boston, where she's visiting me at school, and I leave her locked in the car in the condo parking lot. We discuss this strategy on the drive. If your father's angry, I'll just make him angrier, my mother says.

Better go alone.

Bad Dead Dad is kind of smiling in that manic way.

Our house in Beverly needs a lot of fixing before it will sell. This is what my father says. I imagine this scenario: From the condo in Swampscott, he calls the people who will fix our house in Beverly and then he drives over the bridge to meet them. Maybe he sleeps in our house some nights even though all the furniture's gone because he doesn't like seeing that beautiful city skyline in the slider after all. This is the way buyer's remorse works.

It's nighttime in the condo in Swampscott and my brother's under a table and there's some blood.

A few things need to be taken care of before you can sell your father's house for what it's worth, Realtor says. It's Marblehead, but the walls need painting, the roof needs to be looked at, and there's an encroachment on the property.

My father has to take care of a few things before he can sell our house in Beverly for what he says it's worth. The roof needs to be looked at; the oil burner needs to be replaced. I imagine my father standing beside the oil burner with a wrench but the scenario is implausible.

No, I say firmly. I don't have money for painting, roofs, or dealing with a neighbor's encroaching shed.

My mother says, that oil burner is what gave your brother asthma.

That, and the power plant across the harbor.

When I ask her about this, my mother says, "It wasn't the oil burner, it was the asbestos. And your father never told me. The Realtor told me I needed to fix it before I could sell and I didn't have the money. I'm surprised you don't remember. The duct coming into your brother's room was completely wrapped in it. That's what caused it, the doctors said." I put this part in quotes because this time I was writing down what my mother told me.

It's nighttime in the condo in Swampscott and where's the blood coming from, is my first question. My brother's kneeling on some broken glass that used to be the tabletop, so really he's not hiding under anything anymore.

Your fucking father, my mother says.

Let's think about these questions instead: Where did my father get the money for the condo in Swampscott *before* he sold our house? I ask the two Dead Dads. Mom's cashed-out retirement? No one says anything because none of us knows the answer.

I'd rather sleep beside the oil burner in a house with no furniture than go back to that condo in Swampscott. I'd rather sleep on a mountain of coal. I know this for a fact. A fact.

Did my father miss our house? I ask Good Dad-in-the-Sky. Was he lonely? But Good Dad-in-the-Sky is not my father.

It's nighttime in the condo in Swampscott and, knees and hands? Is that the only blood? I'm asking my brother. My father is standing in front of the front door and how are we getting out of here, is my second question. Just knees and hands? OK.

Good luck, sweetheart.

It's nighttime in the condo in Swampscott and I try to remember standing on the deck in the daytime and looking down, while my father says, look at that skyline, what a view! but I can't remember anything but blue.

Let's think about this question instead: How much did my father pay for the Marblehead house? I ask Good Dad-in-the-Sky. I sit very still and look up to where he is. He sits very still and looks down to where I am.

Aw, you got me, Pal, he says. I don't know any more than you do.

He says Pal like he's my father and I'm little and he's going to lean down and tickle me. Right now, the distance between us isn't very far.

It's nighttime in the condo in Swampscott and I look out to where the ocean would be but all I see is our reflection in the slider. I need to think carefully about this. I think carefully about some prepositions instead: “in,” “under,” “away from.” Brother under the table. Father by the front door. Go out the front door and get in the car, I say to my brother. I drop my keys through the table where the glass isn’t.

How can you be sure about any of this? Good Dad-in-the-Sky and Bad Dead Dad ask me. Sometimes there’s no distinguishing us.

It’s nighttime in the condo in Swampscott and what’s the rest of the story?

Retreat! Retreat!

I’m supposed to be selling my father’s house in Marblehead as quickly as possible for as much money as possible so that I can pay off my father’s debts. And because I’m supposed to be paying the mortgage, which I’m not. We have to do this before they foreclose, Lawyer says. Any day now.

I wanted to get back Mom’s money, I say to the Dead Dads once we all know for sure it will never happen.

It’s nighttime in the condo in Swampscott and my father steps aside and my brother goes out the front door no problem?

Realtor says we should list my father’s house at $579,000 and I say OK because I don’t know anything about housing markets. What happens next?

It’s nighttime in the condo in Swampscott and I’m inside and I want to be outside. Whatever’s going to happen next, my brother’s in the car.

I face the father.

Our house in Beverly sells for $60,000, and $1, and $625,000, and today on Trulia.com I find out our house is for sale for $779,900. I open the slideshow of photos. Our house has a few special features but some of these special features don't add any value so they aren't photographed. And some features, like the coal stove, are only visible in memory, where, once a week a man in a truck delivers coal through a shoot into a special room in the basement. Once a week my mother and I listen for the coal shooshing down and she carries me down to the special room in the basement. I carry My Little Pony to the mountain of coal. I want my pony to climb the mountain. I want to climb the mountain like it's a real mountain but then I get all black. My mother uses the special coal shovel to shovel coal into the special coal pail and then we climb back up to the second floor. Because the pail's heavy we stop on each landing. On the second landing she sits down under the window and holds me in her lap. The beach glass we've collected in jars on the windowsill shines moons of light on our knees. After this, I can smell coal in my nose all day.

Bad Dead Dad: Buy now—Beverly's an expensive and desirable suburb. It's no Beverly Farms but you'll be looking at a profit.

I'm in the selling business, I say. I have this house to sell in Marblehead.

It's nighttime in the condo in Swampscott and there's some blood but no, my brother's in the car and everything's OK. Everything's OK, I say. My father has that manic smile on and we're standing very close together. He seems to be screaming and I seem to be speaking calmly.

The coal stove was removed in 1988 when my parents renovated. After this, we got a pool. We were, my father said, moving up in the world.

Twenty days in, Realtor writes me an email about poor showings in Marblehead. There are fifty-one listings within a one-mile radius of my father's house. Is that a lot? That's a lot. He suggests lowering the price of my father's house to $519,000. OK? OK, I say because I still don't know anything about housing markets. Lawyer says, that may not be low enough but you need to get as much here as you can. My father owes a lot of people a lot of money.

It's nighttime in the condo in Swampscott and on the other side of the glass is the beautiful floating city where I'll be going. My brother's in the car. It's OK. Everything's fine.

Our house in Beverly has a widow's walk, a special feature that is accessed through a trapdoor over my bunk bed. When she's pregnant with me, my mother paints the head of a unicorn on the panel. When I'm old enough, we all get on the top bunk and my father kneels up and pushes on the unicorn like he's a strong man in a circus. Wow, I say. It's not that heavy, my father says and disappears. My room feels like the attic until we open the real attic, where it's wet and smells like attic. Something that looks like woodchips falls down on my comforter and my mother's hair. Bob? she says. OK, he says, come up. Are there bugs up there? I say. There's his flashlight light, then his hand. My mother hands me up and my father and I are kneeling in the crawlspace. Don't move, he says. My mother's in the crawlspace beside us but we're not crawling anywhere. My father's flashlight goes off. Get ready, Pal, he says. There's a crack and then we're flooded with wind and I put my cheek down on whatever it is I'm kneeling on. I'm getting wet and it sounds like someone's screaming, I say. It's only the wind, my mother says, look up. When I do, I'm looking at a square of stars. My father stands up. Stand up, Pal, my father says. My mother takes a fistful of the back of my shirt and when I stand up it just sounds like someone's crying. It smells like ocean up here, I say. We look over the roof of our house and the roofs of the neighbors' houses and down the street. At the end of the street is the ocean. The railing is making my hands wet, I say. It's the ocean, my mother says. Do you see any lights out there? What lights? I say. The lights of ships coming home.

It's nighttime in the condo in Swampscott and the ice cubes in my father's drink are moving around in circles and I still have a choice: slider or front door? My father's face or the reflection of my father's face? The fathers are leaning toward me and the city will be impossible to reach. The beach, if there is a beach, will be impossible to reach.

Does any of this matter now, Pal? Good Dad-in-the-Sky says.

Good Dad-in-the-Sky has never called me Pal until today. Neither of us remembered Pal until now and now I feel like crying.

There are many easy-to-remember things—pony on the coal mountain, unicorn on the ceiling—and there are many hard-to-remember things.

It's OK, I say.

Some things are hard to verify, but on Trulia.com I verify the continued existence of the widow's walk. It's only 3' x 3' and not technically safe to stand on but for me the widow's walk takes up a lot of psychic real estate.

My father reaches down to grab me.

Pony on the coal mountain.

Good luck, sweetheart.

Unicorn on the ceiling.

What's the end of the story?

I get out of there. I don't remember the mechanics. I go out the slider and over the railing and the drop isn't far? There's a beach? It's low tide? I get sand in my sneakers? I wade? My pants get wet? My eyes adjust? I climb the slope wet grass parking lot? I stay where I am? Ice cubes on the carpet? My father holding me? That crunching sound? There's glass under my hand? I scrape my knee? A hole? My father swaying? My father crying? My father never even touches me? I walk right out the front door.

That's it?

I walk right out the front door.

Don't go back, Good Dad-in-the-Sky says. There's an open house at our house in Beverly tomorrow from twelve to two and I'd like to go but now I live in California.

My mother's never gotten over selling our house. I *loved* that house, she says.

Some days, I haven't gotten over it either.

I'm standing in the parking lot and my brother's in the car. Everything's OK. I open the car door. I open the trapdoor. The sound of crying is only a trick of the wind.

Stay up here for a minute, Pal? Good Dad-in-the-Sky says. We're standing close together. Our whole house is below us. When there's no moon, I can see in the dark. We put our hands on the railing and wait for the lights of ships coming home.

The Memory in Question

My friend says, you've got to write about what happened that night in the condo.

Why, Bad Dead Dad says.

I don't remember crap, I say.

You do, my friend says.

◆

What I remember is a conversation with my brother. We're at The Perfect Wife and our father's been dead for a year. It's snowing but not snowing enough that my brother's going to have to go plow. He's friends with the bartender, who's giving us beers. He's friends with the guy shooting pool and the guy feeding the jukebox. He's friends with most of the guys coming in from work and most of the guys leaving the booths in the back with their kids. Everyone's always over here shaking his hand and sometimes they're buying us drinks and sometimes my brother's buying us drinks. He's checking the weather again to make sure about the plowing.

> Remember that time you were at Dad's and he flipped out? I say.
>
> When was he not flipping out, my brother says.

At the condo, I say.

That narrows it down, he says.

The time you were under the table, I say. With the glass.

Someone's shaking my brother's hand and we're getting more beers until it's this guy's turn to shoot and he walks away.

Like you were on the floor in the glass, I say.

I don't remember, he says.

With the broken picture frames? I came in and Mom was in the car?

I can't remember dick, he says.

I think the whole table was shattered, I say. He was drunk.

Obviously, he says. Cheers to that.

Cheers, I say and we lift our beers. How did we get out of there?

What's up, he says to this guy taking a coat off and now they're talking about their accounts up on the mountain and no, not enough snow tonight, time for some drinks.

Who knows, he says once the guy's having the snow conversation with someone else.

That's when you started sleeping with the baseball bat, I say.

Did I actually sleep with it though? he says.

The bartender is asking us if we want Long Trail or something else. We want something else. But none of that IPA shit, my brother's saying.

That was when Mom took us to get the restraining order, I say. But the judge like a dick said restraining orders usually make things worse.

We think about this. I don't know what my brother's seeing but I'm seeing an image of a courthouse like in *Law & Order* and a man sitting up there above my head saying, you don't want to make things worse, do you? Can this memory be true?

So I think we just left? I say. Was it like a real courthouse?

Yeah, I don't remember. I do remember finding the bag of pills at Dad's house later though, he says. Now there's a wicked good childhood memory for you.

Hey you remember something, I say and we cheers our beers again.

First of all, who keeps their pills in an unmarked plastic bag in a linen closet?

First of all, what were you doing in the linen closet? I say.

Dad was probably passed out—what else was I going to do. You never had to go there.

Because I was already all growed up. You called me like, why does Dad have pills in a bag?

And you were like, don't touch them.

I should've been like, put 'em in your purse.

We could've made bank.

Why were we so dumb, I say.

Why was I always there by myself, he says.

That sucked, I say.

Yeah for me, he says.

I know, I say.

◆

When I tell her about the conversation, my friend says, OK but you still have to write the memory.

But what if it didn't happen like I remember, I say.

Who can remember, Bad Dead Dad says.

I can't remember dick, I say and she cracks up.

◆

What I remember is a conversation with my brother. He's on the way to the hospital where our father is dying or already dead. We're unsure about this point but my brother's going to be the one to find out while I'm going to be the one in California.

This drive is fucking long, he says.

It's the middle of the night there and it's my job to keep him awake between Vermont and Boston. We've already talked about what the doctor said and what my father's ex-girlfriend-now-friend said and what we're going to say if what we think is happening is happening.

This blows, I say.

Yeah for me. All you have to do is keep me up, he says. You're not doing a great job by the way.

I can't think of anything, I say.

We've already talked about when I'm going to fly and how he's going to drive home in the morning no matter what's happening and then come back with Mom. I'm lying in bed with all my clothes on.

I keep thinking about good memories of Dad, he says.

I think that's good, I say.

Like I know there was a lot of bad stuff but I can't remember.

I think you're supposed to remember the good things, I say. Now especially.

Yeah but weird things keep popping up.

What things? I say.

I don't know. Like dumb things. Going to that Chinese food place off 128 near the mall, remember that place?

I think just you and Dad used to go there, I say.

Because it was always you and Mom, and me and Dad.

You'd always go get Chinese food.

You'd be at some museum. Dad would get the shrimp with the heads on.

That's when you first started liking those, I say.

And he would cook ribs on the grill.

He was always talking about dry rub. I hated those.

It was so good though, he says.

He used to call you Buddy, I say.

Yeah, he says. And playing darts in the basement.

Dad put up those boards because you were ruining the wall.

I was fucking five, he says. What do you want from me.

You still suck at darts, I say.

You don't know, he says. Also, Salem Willows.

I haven't been to an arcade in a hundred years.

Wintergreen popcorn bars? Who thought of that. Those are probably disgusting now.

They were probably disgusting then.

You loved them, he says.

You loved them, I say.

I kind of want that right now, he says.

We should go there, I say.

◆

I'm trying a new thing, I say. It's called, Remember the Good Things.

OK but you still have to write that memory, my friend says.

You don't, Bad Dead Dad says.

Just pretend you're telling me out loud, she says.

◆

What I remember is standing above my brother. It's nighttime and we're in my father's condo in Swampscott. My father has moved here from the Extended Stay America on Route 1, which I can't drive by without crying. I've been in the condo once before this, in the daytime, when my father wants to show me the view of the Boston skyline from the deck. First it's the ocean, then it's the city. What a view, my father says. What a view, I say. But now I live in that city and my father is pointing at the John Hancock building.

What I remember is standing above my brother in the condo in Swampscott. It feels like the middle of the night but it isn't because my mother and I have just been at a bookstore in the city. A poetry reading. This tells me it's winter; it's dark early. When the reading's over and my mother and I turn on our phones, we've missed a lot of calls from my brother. This is before text messages. What he says to our phones, I don't remember but my father's scaring him. We don't know exactly what my father's done. We don't have a lot of information. One of us calls my brother back but I don't remember. We say, we'll be right there, but I don't remember. We're already in the car. My mother drives out of the city faster than she usually drives, which is fast. Maybe we talk about something but I don't remember until we pull into the parking lot of my father's condo building. I remember there's a big tree in the center of a circular drive. But when I see this lot later, driving by on another day, it's just a square with a bunch of parking spaces, isn't it? Maybe my mother parks underneath a tree on the street but I don't remember. What she says, I remember: If he's angry, I'll just make him angrier. Meaning my father and I know she's right. This is why I go in alone. I don't remember thinking, don't make me go in there alone, but later I'll be mad at her about this point and it will take us years to figure it out but we do. I get out of the car. It's double dark like I'm under the shadow of a big tree. Maybe I'm not sure exactly which door is my father's. Maybe I knock and he lets me in. What I see when the door opens, I don't remember.

What I remember is standing above my brother. He's kneeling under a table that, in my memory, isn't really a table anymore because the glass is shattered. There are some picture frames broken down there too. I know the photos are of me and my brother and that some of them used to have my mother in them but she's been razored out. I can picture her void silhouette because I remember seeing these photos the one time I was here in the daytime. Maybe they were displayed on the antique liquor cabinet, the only piece of my father's furniture I remember because it's in my aunt's kitchen now and for me it takes up a lot of psychic real estate. I remember thinking, as I came inside from the bright light of the deck, that's some psycho-killer shit. And, isn't he embarrassed when his friends come over? And, maybe he only puts these photos out for me.

What I remember is standing above my brother. He's on his hands and knees. How I got from the front door to right here, I can't remember. My father, where is he, must be yelling at us but I can't hear him and I can't see him right now. I'm finding out if my brother is bleeding and/or hurt or hit. If he says anything, I don't remember. If he says, hi. If he says my name. He's not crying and he's not moving. It's like he just happens to be down here in the glass. My father is in the kitchen over my shoulder, my father and his reflection are pacing in the sliding glass door. I have a feeling I'm trying to keep him behind me. I'm trying not to look him in the face. What he's saying I can't hear. How bad my brother is cut I don't remember but it's not bad enough that we're going to need help. Like we're not going to need an ambulance. If I say to myself, this isn't that bad, I don't remember, but I'll say it later and then I'll say no that was scary, and then I'll say no it wasn't that bad. My brother can get up. It's not that bad. I don't remember how I know but we're figuring it out. Maybe I'm trying to look at his hands. I'm trying to look at his face. I'm trying to move his body around like it doesn't belong to him. I'm half kneeling half standing because it seems important to stay sort of standing. I'm not asking what happened here. I'm trying to keep my father out of our line of vision. What I remember is dropping my keys to my brother and saying, go out and get in my car. This is what I remember specifically. It is what I wrote down in a journal and later in a story and later in this book, which, if it wasn't memory, turned it into memory. Because if my mother is in the car, why do I have the keys? And furthermore, was it my car driving through the Callahan Tunnel? Was it me speeding down the Lynnway?

What I remember is standing above my brother. He's in his socks, which are white. And then he's gone. This is like looking at two photographs: My brother's there, my brother's not there. He's out the door. If he gets his sneakers, I don't remember. I think he has sneakers later, in the car, but I don't remember. He's outside getting in the car right now. He's with my mother. He's fine. I don't remember my father trying to stop him. In fact, I can't see my father right now. I can't hear him right now. He doesn't matter. The common metaphor for "relief" is "flood" but it isn't a flood. It's a stillness. I was calm before this but now I'm something else. I remember feeling, now it's fine no matter what.

What I remember is standing close to my father. He's between me and the front door and I could touch the front door that's how close we are but I don't. I'm trying to leave. I don't know how I'm going to leave but I know it's fine no matter what. My brother's in the car. Some stairs are behind me. The shattered table situation is behind me. The sliding glass door is behind me and behind that is the deck and the ocean and maybe a beach. I can smell my father's alcohol body but this memory may be lifted from a hundred other memories. If he's yelling slurring sloshing listing leaning and/or threatening, I don't remember. If he's trying to grab me or hug me, I don't remember. If he's crying, I refuse to remember. I'm speaking calmly. The way you speak to a child. I'm not afraid because I have practice. I've spoken to my father like this a hundred times. I say things like, "It's going to be OK, Dad." "Don't worry, we'll see you soon." Those phrases may be lifted from a hundred other memories but in my voice they feel familiar. I'm not scared when I'm speaking this way, I'm powerful. I probably say, "Don't worry, Dad, we love you." I probably say, "I love you." What happens next, I don't remember. I just walk out the front door?

What I remember is standing in the parking lot underneath the big tree, real or imagined, in a dark that's darker than over there where the car is. Maybe there's a streetlight or a moon because the roof of the car is bright. The windshield is bright. I can't see through it but I know my brother's in there and my mother's in there and then I'm in the car too. I'm not scared, I did fine. I did what I was supposed to do. My mother drives us home, I remember, to our house in Beverly, which, for a few more months, is where we still live.

◆

OK? I say.

OK, Good Dad-in-the-Sky says.

OK, she says.

One Sociopath One Hypochondriac and the Word Trauma

Therapist Four says, your father is a sociopath. We're well into things. She says it like a fact not a revelation. Her office is on the second floor, in a building near the pedestrian mall. It's 2004 and I've moved out of Massachusetts. I've moved to Virginia, to this town called Charlottesville, near this quaint pedestrian mall, where my father is still calling and I am not answering. The point is, away from home. Up there in the North my parents are still mid-divorce and it's been snowing for days whereas here it's sunny. I like walking the pedestrian mall with my sunglasses on then coming to this office because I've decided it's nice to have a change from lying on the bathroom floor. At night I drink everything in my apartment then I throw up for a while then I lie on the bathroom floor. Later I get on the couch and watch *Sex and the City* until it gets dark again. This is OK because I'm in grad school: I don't have many obligations. The nothing-but-time situation that everyone else seems to be enjoying is killing me. I spend at least forty percent of my time on the bathroom floor and forty percent of my time watching TV. I sleep on the floor too; the bedroom is off-limits. The rest of my time is split between sitting at a bar I like, buying beer for later, and driving drunk through town with my sunglasses on. On Wednesdays, I show up at school for two hours then I eat dumplings and walk the pedestrian mall then I'm here for fifty minutes of therapy. Before this I just had Sarah

Jessica Parker but now I have Sarah Jessica Parker and Therapist Four. They're getting me through everything.

Therapist Four says, your father is a sociopath.

I made him sound worse than he is, I say. It's a well-known fact that I'm a hypochondriac. If you mention a disease to me, I have it.

From the bathroom floor, a person doesn't have to think about anything. Throwing up and the stomach feeling that comes after throwing up requires total concentration. Who can think about the boyfriend who went back to his wife, the girlfriend who went back to California, the poems that aren't being written, the books that aren't being read? I call my mother several times a day but who can take a mother's advice to go to the gym, to go for a walk, to join a student group? Who can take the girlfriend's calls? Who can take the father's calls after a year of not taking them? We all know my voicemail is always full.

What a relief.

Therapist Four says, you're experiencing PTSD.

From what? I say to Therapist Four. "Sociopath" is a big word.

I don't know, Therapist Four says, years of being in your family? Your parents' divorce, your father's behavior, your brother almost dying last year? We still haven't talked about your brother almost dying. There's trauma.

I recount in my head all the things I might have told Therapist Four to get us all the way to sociopath. I must've been making a lot of shit up.

Therapist Four is about to recommend I get medicated. Trauma, she will say, can't be overcome by will alone. Your brain needs help.

Medication is a story that will last for many years but it is not this story. When I begin writing this story, I'll say to a friend, I feel like I'm just making things up. I can't remember anything. She'll say, maybe not remembering is the trauma. I hate the word "trauma," I'll say. Everyone's using it. So, she'll say, don't use it.

A Story in Four Voices

: Before we begin. This story is really four stories, each of which remembers my brother's illness and his first hospitalization in the fall of 2002.

Bad Dead Dad: Explain.

: The first story is drawn from an unpublished essay called "The Furnace Man," written by Leigh Perham, my mother, in or around 2005. I've used my mother's story with her permission. This story appears in sans serif type on the left side of the page.

: The second story, in italics, is drawn from an unpublished essay called "The Statue of Grief" that I wrote in 2002 or 2003, when I was twenty-one. The third, in quotations, is drawn from "Ambulance," a poem published in my first book in 2012. These stories appear in the middle of the page.

: The last story, on the right side of the page, is a new story, which I've written around these earlier pieces.

Bad Dead Dad: Anything else
you care to tell us?

:

Bad Dead Dad: Are you sure?

:

◆

It began with an almost imperceptible cough,

and it began with wheezing, my brother, fourteen years old, in a bed in the school nurse's office.

It began with the school nurse calling me after she tried to reach my mother.

It began with the school nurse telling me to take my brother to the local hospital. It began with the phrase, "out of an abundance of caution." She said, call his pediatrician.

It began on the drive to the hospital. I was driving fast out of an abundance of caution. My brother had an albuterol inhaler. Was he talking?

It began in 2002.

This story is my brother's story.

It began when he was admitted to the local hospital. It began when they took us upstairs.

How long until my mother arrived? If she was driving from Vermont where her boyfriend lived, it might have been three hours; whereas, if she was driving from our house or from work, it might have been thirty minutes. The three of us might have arrived at the hospital at almost the same time. Neither of our stories preserves this information.

A bed, a corridor. There we were

my son, fourteen years old, wheeling himself around the corridors of Salem Hospital at four in the afternoon, laughing.

Were we scared?

The school nurse said, just for the night out of an abundance of caution.

At ten o'clock the same night struggling to breathe,

I don't want to read any more.

In her story, my mother has preserved a sense of time. For me, many hours of this day are missing. I remember it was day and then it was night.

My brother is in the corridor. My brother is in the bed. My brother is having trouble lifting his head;

he is ambulanced by a team of intensive care doctors and nurses to the pediatric ICU at Massachusetts General Hospital.

By now, my mother has already had to make several decisions. By now, she has already had to sign paperwork.

Sitting in the ambulance I am vaguely aware that every stoplight through downtown Lynn and onto the expressway into Boston is being held. We are at "Priority One," the EMT informs me.

My brother and I are in the back. There was some discussion about who would ride back here with my brother. I decided or was told to get in back so that's where I am. There's a doctor back here with us. My brother's lying on the gurney and the doctor is busy.

I have my hands on my brother's right arm when I'm not in the way.

Later I'll write a poem about this drive and it is from this poem that many of my memories are drawn:

"I narrate the roads we drive by memory: / 'The coastline north of the airport,' I say, / 'the tunnel beneath the harbor,'"

but of course, I didn't really say coastline.

In my mind I still carry a small collection of images of this drive—the exact positioning of my brother and me in space; his right arm—but the poem has supplanted all narrative.

I was, I remember, saying something.

"I speak as if my voice were a
guidewire"

I didn't shut up.

"If I could see / my mother,
where she sits beside the driver,
/ I'd see how tears can look like
sweat—"

a romantic, though perhaps
accurate, image

"as though she's been running /
some long distance"

Wheeled on a gurney beneath a
maze of fluorescent light bulbs,
his stomach compressing rapidly
as he sucks oxygen from a plastic
mask, he clings to my hand. The
doctors run, so I run.

We run.

Through the automatic doors of
the PICU, attending, resident,
and intern doctors take over with
rubber gloves to connect this boy
who was healthy in the morning
to a wall of monitors, intravenous
medicines, and oxygen tanks.

So far, I don't appear in my mother's story. In my memory, first we are in the ER.

Did my mother write me out at the beginning because she wasn't with us at the beginning? Or because it was narratively efficient? Or is this the most accurate representation of reality? It's worth noting here that my mother is legally alone. It is she who is making all the decisions.

The ER is entered from the ambulance bay through a concrete corridor that feels like a subterranean passageway. Then a system of underground tunnels and bays, curtains opened, curtains closed, beds gowns machinery.

But this is a composite memory built from this night and from the other nights we returned to this ER over the next year. I remember running behind the gurney and I remember running alone. I remember, on other nights, running toward the bay where my mother and brother waited.

That night, my daughter and I learn to read oxygen levels, heart rate, blood pressure, and the all-important CO_2 levels.

Here I appear in my mother's story for the first time.

We grasp quickly that his inability to expel CO_2 is a primary concern to the attending physician—CO_2 levels that become dangerously high cause brain damage or worse.

Here we are a pronoun. It strikes me now that my mother's "we" is generous. It is she who is saying, yes.

When the CO_2 level reaches a certain threshold the monitor flashes red and a corresponding beep sounds at the nurses' station bringing a rush of doctors and nurses to the bedside.

Asthma causes a lack of oxygen and an increase in carbon dioxide levels in the blood. In an attack, the lungs try to open like a doorway. The body will try to take in oxygen any way it can: Tissue will swell and distend, and the carbon dioxide will be unable to escape. I watch the carbon dioxide level on the monitor most frequently: A normal level is below 40. Today we're at 152.

This is my story, which I wrote sometime that year. I am probably describing what I saw on the second day, or the third. But I have no reason to doubt my accuracy in terms of the numbers.

The beeps and alarms are about to become familiar. The numbers matter because we can make them familiar.

From where I'm standing, the machines and numbers are all at close range, easily recorded. I've begun to carry notecards and scraps of paper with me (though I don't write a word when I sit with my journal open) and I print down the names of the medications, their purpose and dosage. I mark everything this way. It seems imperative to write things down, to pace the days by this.

I was, I remember, taking notes. But where are my notecards and scraps of paper?

It's easier for us both, it seems, to start with the numbers and definitions. Where we're going, we don't want to go.

What truth am I interested in confirming?

In my story, the PICU is where we begin, perhaps for narrative efficiency. There's a locked door separating the unit from the hallway; you must intercom to be buzzed in. Though we're on a high floor, there are no windows. There's a nurses' station and, circled around it, beds inside bays separated by curtains. The curtains are often open. The bays are dark except when something bad is happening and, in that case, they're follow-the-light white. My story doesn't preserve the geography but I remember it exactly.

The days became one day and yet we are moving through time.

My daughter and I talk to C.J., working to help him breathe more slowly, but his stomach is sucked in around his rib cage like the skeletal hull of a shipwreck half buried in the sand. And he is thirsty. The doctors and nurses refuse water—only popsicle stick sponges soaked in ice and moved around the inside of his dry mouth. He begs for water then cries from the thirst and the sobs prevent him breathing at all.

I can add nothing to this. I can only tell you that the first time I read this passage I began to cry and it took me four days to begin reading my mother's story again.

I had no memory of the sponges and now I remember them.

This is my brother's story and there's a lot he doesn't remember.

Maybe these are two examples of the brain trying to protect us.

Today I've written: 'Atelectasis: collapsed alveoli in the lungs. Pound on the chest to open. Too much x-ray white.' In a healthy lung x-ray, the tissue is dark, woven in heavy grays and blacks. Light colors mean damage, mean blockage, a minefield of white caught glossy on film.

Mixed metaphors aside, there were x-rays. I remember seeing the pictures and feeling, at first, relieved by all the white space. Someone, I remember, had to explain it to me.

It comforts me that my mother and I sometimes have the same propensity toward romanticism. The figurative image as a means of self-protection, a distancing from feeling.

An x-ray is, of course, a negative.

The night sits and goes on at the same time.

Metaphor is a relief we both need.

The nurses take turns pounding on my brother's chest.

In the morning, a dawn no one can see or experience in the windowless PICU, the Israeli attending talks to me outside the curtained cubicle where C.J. sucks oxygen with all his strength. He speaks slowly as if I am deaf instead of frightened.

At first, I can't read my mother's story without crying whereas I can read my own story with no emotion. Writing a story creates a distance that reading doesn't. Maybe this is why we were both compelled to write our stories and why now, seventeen years later, I am compelled to write this one.

"Last night your son's body fought through the equivalent of running a marathon. He is getting too tired to fight anymore. If I come to you in an hour or a minute and ask you to sign this consent form, I am asking because it is a matter of his life or death. Do you understand?" I nod, choking as if a stopper had been crammed into my throat. The attending is telling me that C.J. will not be able to survive without a ventilator to breathe for him.

My mother and I both understand that the doctors don't want to put my brother on a ventilator. Once this happens, a positive outcome becomes less likely.

Thirty minutes later, alone in the PICU, I sign the consent form.

My mother is alone in the PICU. I'm in my roommate's car and she's driving me out of the city. At some point in the morning, my mother and I must've realized that one of us would have to go back to the first hospital and bring one of our cars to this hospital.

My mother is the mother so she will stay and I will go.

Why do I leave when I do? Do we think nothing is going to change in the hour it will take me to go and come back?

My roommate has pulled over into the breakdown lane. My mother and I are speaking on the phone. I remember saying, yes, sign the form. You're right and you can do this. I'm coming back.

My mother is, legally and practically, alone. My mother has to make, and has made, all the decisions.

I stand at the precipice of his bed, tilted backwards to stretch his throat open. He is terrified—brown eyes darting from me to the circle of doctors around the bed. I tell him softly that the doctors are going to make him sleep so that when he wakes up, he will be able to breathe without struggling anymore.

My mother does this part alone.

She is calm and she doesn't cry. I know this without asking.

"No," he whispers hoarsely. "I don't want to go to sleep. Take me home. I want to go home."

My brother does this part alone.

I am somewhere between Boston and our cars in a parking lot.

"I will take you home as soon as you wake up," I promise. "I will be with you the whole time. I won't leave you."

My mother won't leave us.

"You will wake up and be all better. I love you." The drug takes hold and his eyelids fall shut.

This story is my brother's story
and it is also my mother's.

The attending quickly shoulders me out of the way. One doctor tilts C.J.'s head backwards, the attending slides a plastic tube down the back of his throat, the plastic tube is immediately attached to clear rubber tubes leading to the ventilator, three doctors from pulmonary move the dials on the ventilator to create a green arch from the intake of breath to the expulsion of CO2. Simultaneously doctors insert a mainline intravenous feed into his upper thigh, while others attach tubes and monitors to his chest. I am superfluous and pushed aside on the linoleum floor—I watch. I am so afraid that C.J. felt the paralytic before the coma was induced. He was so scared, and unable to give him what he wanted, I let him down.

All of my mother's decisions are
the right ones.

I walk to the water cooler on the opposite side of the PICU, past the curtained areas where seven other children lie comatose attached to life by tubes and wires as their parents are cemented to the machines.

The girl in the bay beside my brother's will die in a day or two.

The attending allows me to return to C.J.'s beside. All the chaos has passed leaving a helpless little boy—freshly into his first few days of high school, yesterday—now silent, completely paralyzed on a cooling bed. The only sound is the mechanical pull and thunk of the ventilator.

I am somewhere on the highway between a parking lot and Boston and then I am being buzzed back into the PICU. My brother has already been intubated.

My brother's body is silent. A ventilator controls his breathing: His chest moves up and down in measured intervals, twenty-four times each minute. Below the diaphragm, the body seems to be counting, remembering its own timing: His stomach pulses in fast, even beats.

The body has turned into pulse, its only display of motion.

A young resident places her hand on my shoulder. I learn later that it is her job to translate tragedy for the children's parents. "We are doing everything possible for him right now." I look at the marble sheen of his body, stripped naked, as immobile as death.

I touch his neck below the jawbone, vertically beneath his right ear. Pulse is so quick that it forms a lump the size of a thumbprint. I press two fingers against it. His heart is contracting so fast that beat blooms over beat, so fast that you can't count a heart rate. Pulse has solidified, hard like stone, a beach pebble beneath the skin of his neck. The monitor above the bed reads 197.

I remember exactly the lump of pulse in his neck. How you can see it from a distance and what it feels like under my fingers.

"That's the paralytic," she says. "We have also given him an amnesia drug. He will not remember the trauma of being intubated . . ." if he lives, I finish for her.

This story is my brother's story and I hope he doesn't remember it. So why am I writing this?

I watch the graphs of green, red, yellow, and orange lines moving across the computer monitor like self-willed serpents. I understand already that the CO2 levels are dangerously high. I know his blood pressure is horrific and the cooling bed is not abating a body temperature dangerously in excess of 104 degrees.

The monitors, the infusion pumps, the charts in the pediatric ICU—these are the only ways to quantify anything. This is the language I know: heart rate, blood pressure, carbon dioxide level, oxygen saturation, CVP value. The monitor produces these in neon. We watch them. Green, blue, red.

"It's a revolving door," the Israeli attending says in dictionary-perfect English, as he tugs on his gray beard. "The next few hours

will determine whether he will live
through the day."

We'll see the dead girl's family
gather and disperse.

We watch and watch.

I'll feel lucky.

I look at the forced-exhalation curve on the ventilator graph as it slides downhill in green ink. There are now twenty-one ticking machines, each with hanging bags of fluids connected by clear plastic tubes to C.J.'s arms, legs, chest, and throat. I do not know that he is being infused with massive doses of steroids like terbutaline and prednisone yet, but I will learn. I will become an expert on a disease I had never even considered, asthma, and on the best practitioners of its prevention in only a few months.

We don't know and then we do.

Besides the monitor, there are
eighteen IV infusion pumps on the
left of the bed. On the right, the
machine for the ventilator stands

as tall as my shoulders, its crisp black display showing the peaks and valleys of lung volumes. Also on the right is the black cube that controls the cooling blanket, the white box that inflates the leg stockings to prevent blood clots, and the nebulizer, which delivers albuterol in a vapor through the breathing tube. This makes twenty-two pieces of equipment. Every day I count.

Twenty-one, twenty-two, this is not the truth I care about as I cared about it then. Every day I was counting.

My daughter, abandoning any pretense of going to her college classes, helps me through the first day—repeatedly soaking washcloths in Rubbermaid tubs filled with ice water, sponging every available surface of C.J.'s glistening body—our hands becoming raw even as his temperature continues to rise. We soothe dry skin with freezing cloths, touching places an adolescent would never tolerate from his mother, but the heat of his body dries the washcloths in seconds. His forehead is an inferno

and his limbs as dry as brown
leaves—no sweat, no moisture.

When I first read it, I am initially surprised by the construction, "My daughter . . . helps me." But this phrase is accurate: My mother is the only mother among us.

Where is my father?

It's worth noting that I am often equally surprised by my own story. I'm reading it to figure out what's true and what I made up, omitted, or deliberately or inadvertently inflected to create the story I wanted to tell. I've been trying to understand my "I."

This may help to explain my initial feelings about my mother's grammatical construction.

My mother doesn't appear in my story until the second paragraph:

We watch and watch. Mostly my parents and I say nothing. If we speak to each other, we speak in numbers.

It's worth noting that my mother appears in my story as a unit with my father, a construction that is misleading. It's also worth noting that I'm about to make myself the hero of the story, a construction that is misleading if narratively understandable. The first thing is surprising to me; the second isn't.

Is it also worth noting that in the course of three sentences my "we" expands, denoting first two of us and then three of us? Which choices reveal desire and which may be read as simple narrative constructions?

Furthermore: Are narrative constructions ever "simple"? How are desire and construction related?

It is my brother's story that all our stories should crowd around but that is beyond my narrative ability.

I have no memory of my father's arrival. But whenever he arrives, it is accurate to say:

Mostly my parents and I say nothing.

The young resident's role now is to prepare me for the possible eventuality of a heart/lung machine.

My mother and I both understand that if this happens, a good outcome becomes statistically unlikely.

The girl in the next bed was on such a machine and now the girl is dead.

There are several conversations but the decision, if it happens, will be made by my mother.

Where is my father? And what, if any, legal rights does he have in October of 2002?

"This temperature—this CO_2 level cannot be sustained without compromising your son," she says. We sponge him and talk to him. I remember reading somewhere that people in a coma can hear those around them. I keep telling him that he is courageous and a fighter. I tell him that he will be all right, but every time a monitor flashes a red line and a siren sounds at the nurses' station, I believe I am watching him die.

Here is something I don't write about in my story but that I remember clearly: I am certain my brother is not going to die. Maybe this belief is a particular power of the young, or maybe this is an example of my brain trying to protect me. I would go so far as to say, this is my single experience of faith.

"Compromising," as my mother has written, means brain damage. We both know it. No one knows if it's already happened.

The attending does not leave when his shift is over despite two changes to the round-the-clock nurses at the bedside.

I speak to the nurses, I ask them questions. Linda is today's nurse.

I still believe this woman, whose name I didn't remember until I read it in my story, saved my brother's life.

She's on from 7 p.m. to 7 a.m. I like twelve-hour shifts better than eight-hour shifts because you don't have to adjust to another nurse quite so often.

Residents, pulmonary specialists, communicable disease specialists, heart specialists hover around the bed. It is painfully clear that in the best hospital in Boston, perhaps the best hospital in the world, no one is clear why this little boy is losing his battle for life.

My brother's death is unimaginable to me and therefore impossible.

"All I can tell you," says the attending, snapping his clipboard down over the latest printouts from the ventilator, "is that your son is a very sick child right now. We cannot predict what will happen in a few hours. We must wait and see."

Linda stands by the table at the foot of my brother's bed.

"Temperature?" I ask, after she lifts my brother's arm to remove the thermometer.

"103.6," she says. "High but better than earlier, now that we have the cooling blanket."

Neither my mother nor I worried about reproducing conversations in our stories. This is something that today makes me feel uncomfortable even though it is a convention of memoir. So let me say for the record that the conversations in my story are reproductions and/or inventions.

This line of justification is, of course, a slippery slope. Here's a new rule: A metaphor is acceptable if it lightens the tone.

I like her because she explains things; I like her because she tells my brother what she's doing even though he's unconscious.

"There we go, C.J.," she says to him as she injects something into the line running into the artery in his thigh. "I'm flushing your arterial line with saline, and I'm putting in another dose of the steroid to help open up those lungs." She has black hair and deep brown eyes like my brother's when they're open.

At some point in the first days, my mother and I set up a kind of routine. I go home to shower at night. I'm supposed to sleep a few hours and come back in the morning. I rarely sleep and usually come right back. Then my mother goes. She's supposed to sleep a few hours in the morning and come back in the afternoon. I'm not sure she ever sleeps; she usually comes right back. We've tried the unit's family shower, which is in a bathroom off the waiting room and only has cold water, but we must have decided getting out of the hospital is good for both of us. Or maybe someone told us it's good for us so that's what we're doing. With the driving, each of us might be away for a few hours at a time. In a twenty-four-hour period, we spend a lot of time at my brother's bed together and we each spend several hours alone there.

"What are we at for epinephrine?" I ask Linda.

My brother is alone in a medically induced coma. It looks nothing like sleep.

Where is my father?

"0.12," she says, "Where we were last night." She hangs a new IV bag, threads the line through the infusion pump, and enters the dose level. I note the number in my head. I note milliliters, volumes, pressures. The epinephrine keeps his heart rate up, the blood moving through his lungs to gain oxygen as quickly as possible. I think of the channels in the body, the dark veins like hallways with blood pressing through.

This overwrought simile is one I recognize from a poem I was working on at the same time. It suggests I was trying to learn to write. It also suggests I was learning to create distance between myself and feeling, which perhaps explains why I now find metaphor so problematic.

My daughter is able to summon some inner voice that allows her to talk on and on to her brother.

"Hey, C.J. You're doing better and better. I'm skipping out of Victorian Literature today. Good thing I'm here with you instead because I never finished *Gulliver's Travels*. I just couldn't get into that miniature government with all those foolish Lilliputians."

I don't recognize my voice in my mother's story, as I imagine she doesn't recognize her voice in mine. But the class was Victorian Literature. The book was *Hard Times*. I never finished it. In a kind of corollary to my unrestrained romanticism, my story of the PICU, the only writing I produced for the class, begins with an epigraph from Elizabeth Barrett Browning's poem "Grief."

My mother is right about the talking. I was, I remember, saying something. I didn't shut up.

She is more resourceful than I am

My mother's care of me, even as a character in her story, does not surprise me at all.

It says more about her character than anything she or I will ever write.

even though I see her face etched with the same fear as my own.

Her care of me allows me to keep reading her story and to keep writing this one.

What I remember being afraid of, consciously and acutely, is my mother driving back and forth to our house each morning. Shouldn't she be back by now? Isn't she too tired? What will happen to us if something happens to her?

Nowhere do I note this fear in my story. Nor would I have shared this fear with my mother, which perhaps accounts for not writing it down.

Neither of us cries inside the PICU. We save sobbing for the corridor outside the automatic doors and the room inappropriately named the parents' lounge. I would name it a level of Dante's *Inferno*. This is the horrible place where doctors advise parents that the situation inside the PICU has deteriorated beyond their means of combat.

We do not eat or leave except to go to the bathroom.

I don't remember crying. Not in the hall, not in the waiting room, not in my car. But this is surprising because I am a good crier and I still cry often.

My father, too, cried often. I have specific and general memories of watching him cry.

When my father cries, he looks down at his hands, which he fists on his stomach. He stands blanched by the hallway fluorescents. His eyes are wide. Tears form, build, and cut across his cheeks, which are flattened gray. He doesn't make a sound when he cries. His body is still as a mountain.

My father makes his appearance in my story early on even though in the first days in the hospital, a time that seemed to both pass and to become one indefinite moment, I have no memory of him. Was my story trying to correct his absence?

Furthermore: Was it the story that allowed me, years later, to write the end of this poem?

"I bring my father to the poem only / suddenly, to amend the law of his absence, / and because my brother's eyes are closed."

My father appears in my mother's story much later than he does in mine. The chronology she presents is, I think, more or less accurate. But in both stories, my father eventually has his narrative entrance.

He's shaved his beard off; I hadn't immediately recognized him when he first came to the hospital. I don't go up to him in the hallway; I don't stand by him beside my brother's bed. We haven't spoken in three months.

The feeling of not recognizing my father is both accurate and familiar. I have experienced it on more than one occasion. But I don't know if it is accurate to say that my father and I stopped speaking three months before this. Our chronology is something I've been trying to figure out. Rather than finding this detail reassuring, a piece of our historical record preserved, I find it suspect. For one thing, I have memories of my father at my college graduation months later. So, if indeed we weren't speaking in the hospital, our separation was neither complete nor permanent.

The law of superposition might be useful here. Can we reconstruct a reliable narrative of the past by excavating the strata of memory? And even if we attempt to preserve the temporal relationships of the memories we have, what about the memories we don't have, the ones that are missing from our stratigraphic sequence? Without these memories, is it still possible to determine causality, to posit any narrative at all?

That I might be making things up in my writing—that I might be lying—then or now, consciously, or unconsciously, is one of my big fears.

Neither my understanding of the conventions of memoir nor of the subjective nature of memory does anything to lessen this fear.

I watch them both cry. I haven't cried at all and this surprises me. As a rule, I'm good at crying, while my mother I've seen cry only once in my life. This was before my brother was born. I had come up the stairs to my room after school and she was sitting in the dark of my closet underneath my dresses and coats. Plastic dry-cleaning bags swung around her like vines from some foreign rainforest. I remember standing back, not sure if she knew I was there, not sure if I should speak. Suddenly, as quick as a storm would come up from the beach by our house, my father was in the doorway, blocking the hall light. He looked at me and didn't step into the room. Without saying anything, I walked to my mother. I molded my body against her back. At some point, my father must have gone. I'm not sure how long it was that my mother and I sat in the closet. I remember finally she picked me up and carried me back downstairs into the lit house.

Similes aside, this event was both shocking and terrifying. Though I have represented it here as a narrative, for me this memory consists of a feeling bound with an image. My mother in a closet, me outside it, a dark room, somewhere a light, the suggestion of my father. If I could separate this memory from language, it would exist outside of narrative time: a lyric memory.

Unfortunately, the law of superposition doesn't hold when it comes to memory: All my stratigraphic sequences are deformed.

The past often feels like the present.

When my mother cries, she weeps full, loud sobs. I'm afraid for her body; the lines of her trachea and esophagus press visibly through the skin on her neck. I wonder how much it takes for a body to come apart, ribs simply coming open and undoing themselves, unfurling like the walls of a house might in an earthquake.

Romanticism aside, I was, consciously and acutely, afraid for my mother's body. She had been losing weight steadily as her divorce from my father went on for months and then for years.

Over the last months, I'd guess my mother has lost close to forty pounds though she was always slender.

I was afraid my mother was going to die.

Her jeans are a size two, but she stands with her thumb hooked through the belt loop, holding them up. They gap around the hips, around her front where the hill of the stomach should be.

This fear was confirmed when a friend of my mother's, a nurse who worked in a different unit of the hospital, visited us. Standing outside the PICU, she tells me it looks like my mother is going to die.

Sometimes, because I am unable to say anything else, I report new dosage levels to my mother when we're standing outside the PICU.

I tell her levels in milliliters, in micrograms. She doesn't keep track; she doesn't register the names of the medications or their uses.

The characterization of my mother is inflected. Though I remember she looked dazed and faraway, as though her self had been pushed down inside her body where I could not reach it, my mother was keeping track of a lot of things. This inflection is another kind of lie, and it makes me feel ashamed.

What details am I inflecting now?

All of them.

The more interesting question might be this one: Why, in 2003, did I inflect my details to make my mother appear weak?

Common sense would say this: Because I was afraid for her, I was mad at her. Common sense would say, I wanted her to take care of me. I remember feeling neither of these things but, common sense would say, that is to be expected.

The brain tells a story of its own.

My story attempts two moments of connection. The first, perhaps unsurprisingly, occurs with my mother. In this scene, I give her an apple:

Someone tells me this is the kind of food you bring to a hospital, so I do. My mother sits on the side of our cot and I hold the apple up to her mouth. She bites down, just through the surface, and I turn the apple in my hand to present the new skin to her. She turns away.

"I'll throw up," she says. And I believe her, so I wrap the apple up in a paper towel and put it back in the plastic supermarket bag. She lies down on the bed and sobs. I leave because I don't know what else to do, because I cannot comfort her.

Setting aside the obvious symbolism of the apple, it's still embarrassing to admit that in the second scene I give my father (surprise) an apple:

In the hall, my father paces. He carries his coat everywhere with him in his arms. My mother and I have taken the room with the cot so it occurs to me that he has nowhere to set it down. I feel like I should offer to take it, to put it on the floor of the room in the pile of my clothes. But I don't know how to ask for the coat, to admit to recognizing that he's been carrying it, and I don't know if it's OK to put it in the room with my mother sobbing.

"An apple," I say and hold it out to him.

Happily, this parallel construction is, from this distance, sort of funny.

I've picked the one that seems the least bruised; I've polished it on my sleeve. I'm embarrassed that I can manage only the name, that I can think of no way to say anything else.

"I don't want it," he says.

"You haven't eaten today."

"I probably won't eat it, you know," he says.

"It doesn't matter, eat what you want, throw it away." He takes the apple and bites into it. It takes him a long time to swallow each mouthful. I think he might begin to cry again. I don't want to stay and watch this. I don't want to know that he cries. I feel like I could prevent him from crying if I do the right thing. I stand there for a few more seconds. He looks down at his hands and I walk back to the PICU, press the buzzer to be admitted, and the double doors swing open.

Both of these scenes are, I think, lies. I say "I think" not to be generous to my twenty-one-year-old self but because I'm not sure. I have a feeling.

Let's go back to what I do remember: In the hospital cafeteria I fed my mother half of a grilled cheese sandwich every day. It's accurate to say that on many days I held the grilled cheese sandwich up to her mouth, and that on many days she said she would throw up.

I remember my father with his coat in his arms. I remember my father chewing. These things must be true because reading them, even now, makes me feel ashamed. A truth, it seems, has as much power to shame as a lie. I could not help him.

Here are some possible explanations/rationalizations: There was an apple but I don't remember it now. I thought grilled cheese wasn't as poetic as an apple. I wanted to share something with my parents so I invented something. I wanted to connect my parents to each other by proxy of the apple. I felt alone, and I felt that each of us felt alone, and I tried to fix it. Was I aware of any of this when I was writing?

As a child, you know something. You know and you're good at watching.

I've spent a lot of time trying to understand where and why my story is incorrect even though I knew at the beginning that this could never be done with any certainty.

Writing tells a story of its own.

At night, I shift through the halls; doors on the PICU floor are always closed.

I've started to feel a lot of affection for my twenty-one-year-old "I." Was she aware that what she wrote would turn into what I remember?

The halls are this kind of shiny white, like fields after snow—close-up you see the blemish of dirt, of thistle and grasses; but from far away, the distance, say, of memory, you have a single monumental color. I sit down and put my back against the wall. I open a notebook. I want any distance, the distance maybe of ten years—I'd be in a new city then, a new house.

And here I am. New city, new house.

And here I am trying to go back.

Leaving is too frightening. Pushing the black handle to generate the electronic swish outward of the PICU doors stops your heart in dread of what you might find has occurred on the other side while you were gone for ten minutes.

My mother's story exists primarily in narrative time whereas my story exists primarily in lyric time. In her story we have a sense of moving through and in my story we have a sense of standing still. Both sensations are accurate.

We circle my son's bed like lions on the prowl eager to suck up computer-generated information that links us to C.J.'s silenced mind. Dark eyelashes rest on glistening brown cheeks and his expressive arched eyebrows have become placid.

In his hospital bed, his curls have begun to mat because he's been lying on his back. I stand beside the bed and lean my elbows on the sheet next to his shoulders. The tube in his throat connects to a port where three plastic hoses spider out across his body and attach to the various machines. I'm used to the tubes; I scoop them off his shoulder so I can put my hands on his arm.

Here my brother and I are alone.
Here I've written my parents out.

My vocabulary comes from Linda: She writes the names of the medications on strips of surgical tape and attaches them to the IV infusion pumps. Versed, fentanyl, vecuronium, steroid, terbutaline. I gather the types of machines and medications like constants, like stones. I need them.

It's possible to erase things in conscious and unconscious ways: through narrative choice, inflected detail, metaphorization, remembering selectively and not remembering, lying, and by prioritizing one feeling over another. This is a partial list. But the last example may be instructive: It's possible, even plausible, to say that when I was in the hospital, I felt alone without consciously feeling anything. Maybe this is what my "I" was trying to tell me. It must be noted that she was, with her heavy-handed similes and symbols, practically beating me over the head with this information.

He is so motionless beneath the tubes and wires that our only link to the beat of his heart is the blip on the monitor screen. The respirator that has become his lifeline is a mechanical rhythm to which we adhere like addicts.

When she's in the PICU, *she puts her face inches above C.J.'s face and whispers to him. She doesn't watch the machines; she doesn't ask Linda questions. Sometimes she nods and looks past me when I tell her his blood pressure is 180/98 (too high) or his oxygen saturation is 88 (too low). Sometimes she can't listen to me at all; my language is foreign, something she doesn't want to learn.*

'Tender shepherd, tender
shepherd—'

I find myself singing the songs I used to sing to him when he was a toddler—"Tender Shepherd" from *Peter Pan*—over and over again, whispered into his burning ear. When I sing the words, his heart rate steadies and his blood pressure drops. I sing hour after hour, my sneakers sticking to hospital fluids—urine or lymphatic ooze—mopped into the linoleum floor.

'Tender shepherd, tender
shepherd—'

By nightfall forty-eight hours later, a sundown unknown in the microcosm of the blind intensive care unit, we are functioning on adrenaline only. Time moves not at all, but our clothes deteriorate in sweat and grime as the hours tick away. We have lost the ability to comfort each other and the thunk of the ventilator expels air from our lungs in unison.

'Fast asleep, fast asleep—'

My mother sings for hours and then days.

The repetition comforts me too.

When it is very late, we undress in the room they've given us to sleep in. The room has a fluorescent light, a television, and a cot. You can barely fit to walk between the side of the bed and the wall.

My mother and I each had our own superstitions though we didn't talk about them and they don't appear in our stories. I had my brother's Discman, his two CDs, John Mayer and Counting Crows, and the silver chain he'd worn to school. I listened to the albums at night, on my brother's headphones, lying on the cot. That year, I would listen to no other music. I drove with my car radio off. If a song came on in a room unexpectedly, I left the room. I wore the chain everywhere. I still keep it with my jewelry.

Repetition is a kind of superstition.

We always leave the TV on at night. Otherwise the room seals up, like the lower cabins of a ship, airtight and black.

The blackness I remember. The suction sound I remember. When the door closed, the room sealed.

Or, like a tomb, I imagine. But I don't say this to my mother. We get in the bed side by side and I put my arm across her waist. We don't speak. I'm afraid to put my head against her shoulder, although I want to.

I don't remember us touching. I have no memory of wanting to put my head on her shoulder.

I did, however, want my mother to read my story, which I began writing during or soon after those days in the PICU. I sent it to her as soon as I finished it. She didn't criticize my characterization of her. She didn't criticize at all: She was full of praise. And when my story won a prize in a student essay competition, she was the one to come with me to New York to accept it.

What was each of us trying to feel, and not feel, by writing our stories? What was each of us hoping the other would feel by reading?

When I read it now, my mother's writing of me feels accurate whereas my writing of her feels inaccurate.

Were both of us trying, also, to feel something about my father?

Well, I'm still trying.

Someone, a friend perhaps, has called my ex-husband. He hovers in business clothes ten feet from the bedside, unable to touch the still body of the son he never touched at home. Unable to find words to speak—perhaps to his son, perhaps in front of his daughter and ex-wife—he instead talks to doctors. He wants to blame the divorce for this illness. He wants to blame me. I do not know about asthma yet. Could the stress of the divorce have taken an innocent child and placed his life in such extreme danger?

Some of the details are inflected but they speak to things I remember. There was a time in the PICU when neither of my parents was allowed to see my brother. A few hours, a day, two days? This was, as I remember it, a result of something my father said to a doctor about my mother. It may also have been because my brother seemed to do worse when my father was present, or when my parents were present together, but this is only a feeling. I have no medical evidence to support it. A social worker was brought in to speak to each of my parents individually. I sat beside my brother and waited. It may be that the outcome was that my father was not allowed to see my brother for some period of time. Or it may be that my father, by his own choice, visited for an hour or two each day and even then stayed mostly away from the bed, and from us. Or we from him.

I have two particular memories of my father from this time. The strongest memory occurs in the parking garage when, one day, my father paid for my parking. It is one of my favorite memories I have of my father. In whatever brief exchange we had, we were kind to each other.

The other memory is one I share with my mother. We both remember my father leaving the PICU to host a Super Bowl party though this detail appears in neither of our stories. This happened, we remember, when no one was sure if my brother would live. But this memory, though—or perhaps because—we share it, is almost certainly inaccurate. My brother was on a ventilator in the PICU in October; the Super Bowl is in February. My father must have left for another reason. Or, he must have left for a Super Bowl during a different hospitalization. My mother and I are collectively confusing two memories, or we have collectively invented this memory.

"It wasn't the Super Bowl," my mother says when I call her up to confirm our invented memory. "Your father had Celtics tickets."

So I invented our invention of the memory? And believed it for twenty years? And wrote it as though it were true? Oh.

But is my memory of this "we" wholly inaccurate? Was there a story my mother and I were both trying to tell?

My mother's story of the PICU is framed by a second story, her story of my father's alcoholism and their divorce. My story, too, includes a second story, the story of my father's alcoholism and our estrangement.

Here's something Grace Paley didn't say based on something she did say: 'A story is not a story until it's two stories.' I always misquote her because I never remember the actual quote and because I prefer my made-up version.

As a writer, maybe as a human, I am not capable of parsing our second stories at the same time as this one. But it's accurate to say that separating them is misleading.

There was talk among the doctors about what, medically, my parents' divorce could or could not cause. And soon there would be testing for concrete causes—for allergens in the pigment used to paint the white lines of the high school football field, for example.

Must one story always be prioritized over another?

There were never any answers.

On the third day, dehumanized and lifeless in the medical mechanical world of the PICU, my son's fever broke. The attending, cautiously optimistic, went wherever intensive care doctors go to sleep. Glued to stools provided by the gregarious nurse with Winnie the Pooh characters printed across the scrubs stretched tight over her wide stomach, my daughter and I nod off and jerk awake as the monitors blip and the ventilator pulls up C.J.'s rib cage and releases it with a predestined thud. The smiling nurse brings us tea and crackers, while she translates intravenous labels and changes infected IV sites in arms and legs.

In this writing I have preserved the first pages of my mother's story exactly, chronologically, and with no omissions. I have sewn my younger self's story and her poem, out of order and with omissions, around my mother's story. I should say that this is because my mother's story presents a coherent narrative, which has been helpful to me in writing this one. I should also say that in many ways her story makes more sense to me than my own.

It's tempting to read this as a metaphor for our relationship.

Though we will still be days in the PICU, my brother will one day be extubated. We will one day be moved upstairs to another unit, one with windows, where it will be possible to tell night from day. And—though my brother will be admitted again to this hospital and to other hospitals, and though we won't know it for years—the worst of his illness is over.

Two stories are going to be written. Then a third and a fourth. Each of them will circle the others and the two stories that remain unwritten. One belongs to my brother and one belongs to my father.

The Personal Essay: Round One

I'm putting us in a story, I say to the Dead Dads. A certain kind of story. A personal essay.

An essay like for school? the Dead Dads say. Aren't you a little old? They're in good spirits.

We're visiting my mother in Vermont, which is where she lives now. This used to be her parents' house and when I was a child we stayed here on weekends. We're watching the sunrise, which we never do, except I'm writing this personal essay.

Good spirits, Good Dad-in-the-Sky says. Get it?

Bad Dead Dad: What's it about?

The mountains turn blue then purple.

It looks like heaven out there, Good Dad-in-the-Sky says.

Executors and foreclosures, I say. And illnesses.

And death, Bad Dead Dad says.

And not remembering.

I wonder if I'll have the three of us inside my head forever.

Outside is the yard and the goldenrod is in its last bloom. Beyond that is the apple orchard. None of the trees produce fruit anymore. The mountains turn purple then green. When the goldenrod dies, my allergies will clear up.

What do you see out there? the Dead Dads want to know. They're sitting at my feet. They're wearing pajamas. Because I can't remember my father in pajamas, I have to make something up: sweatpants and Patriots T-shirts.

Good Dad-in-the-Sky: Can you see our tree?

We're remembering the summer my father spent resurrecting one of the apple trees when this house still belonged to my grandparents and my father was still alive. My father's out there watering and Miracle-Gro-ing and pruning and mowing. Once the field grass turns into lawn I'm sitting under the branches, playing with the bow and arrow I've been making from a dead branch and some twine. Whatcha gonna shoot, Pal? my father says. I tighten the twine but I can't get the bow to shoot the dead-stick arrows I've notched with a kitchen knife. Nothing, I say.

I can still feel the grass under my feet, Good Dad-in-the-Sky says. We look at his soles, which turn brown. He picks off bits of leaf and twig.

I don't want the Dead Dads to know that someone bought the orchard and planted pine trees along the border with the yard and now the pine trees are ten years old and twenty feet tall and it's hard to see the apple tree at all.

Good Dad-in-the-Sky: Why pine trees?

The new neighbor doesn't want to see this little house when she drives up her driveway to her big house. She calls this the trailer park.

Good Dad-in-the-Sky: I can just see her McMansion now.

Bad Dead Dad: I want to see my tree.

I want to know if my father looked for his tree when he was in this yard last, a few months before he died. When we were all here for my brother's rehearsal dinner. I want to know if, before he died, he remembered the tree. But any talk of my brother's wedding might divide the Dead Dads and right now we're all on the same page.

Good Dad-in-the-Sky: A pun!

I'm not ready to talk about the wedding, I say to the Dead Dads.

That's OK, Good Dad-in-the-Sky says.

Why does a tree have to represent anything?

Bad Dead Dad: Don't go there.

But now I'm having a hard time seeing anything out this window.

So this essay, this "personal" essay, how personal is it? Bad Dead Dad says.

Personal, I say. Why can't I remember my father's pajamas?

Bad Dead Dad: I thought we didn't write personal essays.

We don't, I say.

Can we get some coffee for this conversation?

This morning Good Dad-in-the-Sky and Bad Dead Dad are using the same tone of voice. It's the tone of voice that says no one's planning to yell at me. The tone of voice that might offer to take me to Dunkin' Donuts.

Let's go to Dunkin' Donuts, the Dead Dads say. Let's put the top down like we used to. What a day!

I wonder if I'll have you both inside my head forever, I say, or if you'll go away when this is over.

Coffee, Good Dad-in-the-Sky says. Then we'll dive into family history.

I don't want us to go away, Bad Dead Dad says.

The Dark Wood

I'd like to leave the living out of it. The dead belong to me.

The living retain certain rights of consent. Neither my brother nor my mother consented to appear in this story. It comforts me to know that in many ways they do not appear. The only things that appear in this story are the things of my creation. My real brother and my real mother are not my creations. They are out there right now living in another time zone; right now they are probably going to bed. My brother is repositioning his sleeping baby to make a space to lie down. My mother has fallen asleep on the couch watching BBC America. That's what I imagine. It might be happening right now just this way. The fact that they are out there not being my creations comforts me.

My brother and my mother are out there right now. It makes me happy to think of it and I'd like to let them go to bed in my imagination.

My brother and my mother will, perhaps, be unhappy when they see the creations that bear their names in this story. Likely, they will be unhappy. When I tell her what I'm writing, my mother says, oh god, I'm going to be the bad guy in the story, aren't I.

Actually, she doesn't say that. We're sitting with our backs up against a closet door because we like to read here in the late afternoon when I'm visiting her, on the upstairs carpet in the square of sun that comes in her west-facing windows. My mother says something something bad guy, while my mother-creation says, oh god, I'm going to be the bad guy in the story, aren't I.

In this story, where I have to create everything, things get complicated.

On the other hand, certain things have become simpler.

Once there were two fathers: my father and my father-creation. Things were tricky back then. For one thing, my father was alive, so my father-creation was always smacking into him. Who is *that*? the father-creation would say. Sometimes my father would do what we expected him to do and sometimes my father would not do what we expected him to do.

This could be why I didn't talk to my father for many years, so many years that by the time I did speak to him, he was a different person. My father-creation no longer resembled my father at all. For one thing, my father was sick. Sometimes he didn't remember my name, whereas my father-creation was still the same old bad guy.

Much of what happened or could've happened between my father and me after that was disrupted by my father-creation. Go away, I said to my father-creation. I'm done with you. Ha, he said. And that was that.

Now the only father I have is my father-creation. To deal with this, I've surgeried the father-creation into a holy trinity: Good Dad-in-the-Sky, Bad Dead Dad, and "my father." Here they are in the story. To get them here, I had to make certain structural decisions.

Remember your birthday parties, my mother says when I tell her what I'm writing. Just remember those birthday parties every time I'm about to be the bad guy.

We both close our books and I lie down in the sun square.

I do remember. My mother took the legs off the dining room table and covered it with a tablecloth. On the table were noisemakers and yo-yos and wax lips and Hoodsies. One of these birthdays was a Teddy Bear Picnic in which my teddy bears, with happy birthday balloons tied around each furry wrist, sat in the center of the table. *If you go out in the woods tonight, you're in for a big surprise. For all the bears that ever there was are here tonight because because tonight's the night the teddy bears have their picnic.* That's the song. Every kid I knew came with presents and we sat around the table my mother made just the right height for us. I remember my birthdays and they are all happy memories. Most of my memories are happy memories.

Bad Dead Dad: So what happened?

Most of my childhood memories are happy memories and most of my happy memories contain my mother. Of all the problems my mother and I have had, absence is not one of them.

Of all the problems my father-creation and I have had, absence is also not one of them. With my father, absence is everything.

Bad Dead Dad: You lived with your father until you were eighteen years old.

True.

In every true story I told myself for many years, the father-creation was the bad guy. The father-creation was doing all kinds of bad-guy things: for example, calling my cell phone as I stood on the commuter-rail platform and saying, I know where you are, I'm looking at you right now out the window of my car. In this example, the father-creation resembled the father exactly.

Every story needs a good guy and a bad guy.

The father-creation was thinking all kinds of bad-guy thoughts: I will come to your house, I know where you live, you can't hide from me, you ungrateful bitch, I will find you. In this example, the father-creation may or may not have resembled the father. In this example, the father-creation may have resembled only my own fears.

I have no way of knowing what my father was thinking as he circled his car around the train station.

Sitting there in his car, the father might have been thinking, I miss you.

For many years I told these father-creation stories to therapists and friends and teachers and to strangers in bars when I was drinking. I also told these stories in poems. In this way, the father-creation fathered the I-creation. There we were in a story together.

Even before my father died, I was starting to be unclear about which of my true stories were true. Even then, when I told myself the story of the phone call on the commuter-rail platform, the father-creation was often thinking these other thoughts: Stay on the phone, Pal, please, why have you cut me out of your life?

But I had to admit to the possibility that my father-creation still may not have resembled my father. In this example, the father-creation may have resembled only my own desires.

Bad guy, good guy, which guy was he and which guy was I? Bad guy, good guy, at least we were in the story together.

It's easy enough to turn my mother into the bad guy if I need one for this story. In the first place, this is a matter of craft: The mother-creation is a convenient figure against which the I-creation can act. See the third definition of "craft" in the *Oxford English Dictionary*: *Skill used in deceiving others.*

If you go out in the woods tonight—

In the second place, this is a testament to the relationship I have with my mother: She will bear the mother-creation that bears her name and she will still love me.

On the other hand, I am not entirely sure my father loved me. Or maybe it is more accurate to say, my father loved me in a complicated way.

Is this why you're dragging us through all this? Bad Dead Dad says. How do you know what's accurate?

I'm entirely sure of one thing: The father-creation did not love me. He stayed up all night drinking, thinking, bad daughter, the no-good bitch of a daughter who never calls, not even when he's sick, not even when he's in the hospital, in the hospital for the fifth time this year, in the ICU, not even then, not even intubated, not even when he's nearly dying, he's dying and the daughter doesn't care, doesn't come, doesn't get there until he's dead. He's dead and still the daughter is not there.

The father-creation is also thinking, I missed you. Pal, I miss you.

The daughter does not love him. The daughter loves him.

In the minutes after my father's death, the father-creation and I are buoyed together in a sudden sea. It's floating here we begin to notice we have no idea what the true story is. It's floating here we begin to realize that the father, being dead, has no power to reveal anything to us.

If you go out in the woods tonight, you're in for a big surprise—

At this point in the story, I wish for my mother. Because the story is mine, she appears, as she will always appear. She appears after sundown and before there's a moon, when the lit square of carpet disappears and the woods in the windows are darkest.

I don't think I can write it anyway, I say.

You can, she says.

An Education

The daughter's car is about to be repossessed. She receives some paperwork in her dorm mailbox. Maybe the paperwork was sent to the father first, who was making the payments up until now because she's an undergraduate, or up until, it seems now, many months ago. Maybe the father threw the letters away. This letter implies there have been many earlier letters. Many attempts, this letter says. Maybe there were registered letters. Maybe the father signed and maybe the father shredded. Maybe the father stood over the shredder in the corner of his office. Maybe the father laughed. The father knew, certainly, that he had stopped sending any payments. Maybe the collection agency has just now managed to track the daughter down. Why didn't the father tell the daughter? This is what the daughter thinks looking at the letter. Why didn't the father tell her he was not sending any more payments? If she had known sooner she could have gotten another job. She's working at the slide library on campus for $6 an hour but she could also be a waitress. She has a friend who works at Bertucci's and she could work at Bertucci's. It's late in the game, the daughter's finding out. The daughter is looking at a big number. A big number at the bottom of the letter. She could have been working at Bertucci's all this time. How many hours at the slide library will it take to—? The daughter is having a hard time understanding fees and consequences. She will need more hours. Tomorrow she will go to the slide library and request them. The daughter is starting to feel a panic attack coming. This is a feeling she's used to. Tomorrow she will ask her friend about Bertucci's. Pretty soon she'll be on the floor underneath the mailboxes unless she gets going. The daughter's name at the top of the letter. The father's address at the top of the letter. Didn't she sign the paperwork for this car? The daughter still has time to make it to the common room. And wasn't her father only a cosigner? Wasn't that the deal? Before she blacks out. The roommate will say, wake up, it happened again. Or some stranger will say, dude, what happened? And when the daughter, leaning over the desk of the car dealer, a man her father seemed to know, a man she was afraid to talk to, thought, this isn't a good idea, before she and the father signed their names on parallel lines, shouldn't she have listened to herself? But no, she thought instead, selfish consumer that she is, I really need a car. She thought, because otherwise how will I get home? Home is where the mother is. The dorm has many stairs. And didn't the father say, this is just a formality? Didn't the father say, of course I'll be making the payments until you graduate? Didn't he say that? But why should he, the father, pay for the car? It's her car, after all, and she's been driving it. And hasn't she been lucky, after all, to have all of these things paid for, things like this car, things many of her other friends don't have paid for? The dorm has many hallways. The friend who works at Bertucci's, for example. Shouldn't the daughter, after all, thank the father? She's gotten a year of free car payments. She's won the car lottery. Shouldn't she be grateful? The father is not responsible for this, why should he be? Couldn't she, at least, pretend to be grateful? The hallways look all alike. But she won't even talk to him. Shouldn't she be calling him up, right now, thanking him? But no, she is not answering his calls, she is not answering any calls, she has the roommate answer the phone or, in the room alone, she gets way down under the comforter and waits the ringing out. The daughter will never pick up a phone again. This is a pact she has with herself. This is a pact she will keep. On the other end of the phone it is always the father. The daughter has taken the wrong hallway. The daughter is on the wrong floor. Sometimes the father has that voice, that particular father voice she hates, the "selfish bitch" father voice, and sometimes the father is crying, and sometimes weeping, and sometimes the father is on the voicemail saying, Call Me Back. And when the daughter doesn't call back, the father shows up, his car idles outside the dorm, this happens every week, and the daughter never goes out there, does she? She could go out and lean in the window of his car, couldn't she? Hi, Dad, she could say. She could let her dad take her to dinner, couldn't she? She could get in his car and say soothing things, couldn't she? But no, when the roommate says, the Jaguar's back, and the daughter pictures the father down there in the green luxury of waiting, she doesn't go outside that night. She doesn't go outside the next day. She skips her classes. She doesn't show up at the slide library. But if she had just put her hoodie on instead, if she had put the lanyard with the keys over her head, if she had gone downstairs, gone out to his car in the dark at the curb, his window rolling down, hi, Dad, if she had gotten in, buckled into the soft seats the lightest color of pantyhose, her father running the heater, breathy, teary, drunk?, no, the daughter never thinks he's drunk. She decided, when she was fifteen and a half and driving his car without a license to get her brother from soccer practice while he sat next to her swearing, not to imagine him drunk in a car ever again. And still, despite this, she could have sucked it up and sat there next to him for a few minutes, in his car, a parked car, a car at a curb, easy, she could've sat there breathing the humid heater air. And she could have said, while it snowed and the windshield gummed with his breath, I'm here, Dad, it's OK, don't cry, and also, I'm grateful for the car, thank you, I'm grateful for everything, all of it. And if she had done this, could what happens next have been avoided? Could it have been avoided, the father getting out of the car, the father in a wool coat, waiting on the steps in the snow, the father saying to someone, my daughter lives here, and someone opening the door, letting him in, though wasn't there a warning when they were freshmen, weren't they told, the first week of school, don't let anyone in the dorm behind you, it doesn't matter what anyone says to you, don't believe them, the father beside the mailboxes, the father walking each hallway, first floor, second floor, it doesn't matter what anyone says, don't believe it, common room, the quiet nighttime couches, make sure no one follows you, the communal bathroom where girls are showering, steam, is that his daughter, is that her, until here he is on the third floor, the daughter's name on a whiteboard, could it have been avoided, would he be here, now, standing at her door?

Cells That Wire Together Fire Together

The mother, besides being the mother, is the big kids' teacher and everyone's principal. The daughter is a little kid and she's supposed to be napping down here with the little kids. The naptime teachers have her down on the smelly mat. They have her shoes off. They know she's a flight risk. The naptime classroom on the dark side of the building is the darkest classroom of all. The mother's classroom is at the other end of the long elementary hall. The mother's blackboard has a timeline of kings and conquerors in colored chalk. In her imagination, the daughter hears the mother's pen clicking on and off. The daughter hears the mother's sneakers squeaking on linoleum. The daughter is sweating under the blanket. The big kids have their hands up. The daughter knows where the mother is and what she is doing but knowing isn't enough. The daughter conjures the hall and the closed classroom doors. She'll be running up the bright white path of the reflecting fluorescents. She's running as fast as she can in socks. If the naptime teachers catch her they carry her back to her mat but if she makes it to the mother's classroom they stand in the doorway and shrug their shoulders. The mother never sends the daughter back. To the daughter this is a matter of life and death every day. Either she will be caught or she will be lucky. Either she will sit at her mother's feet or

Try writing about yourself in the third person, the daughter tells her students again and again. The daughter, besides being a daughter, has become a teacher. Why? the students want to know, why? Sometimes it's easier to imagine things that way, she says. But we're not imagining things, the students say, this is a nonfiction class. You're either telling the truth or

The daughter calls up the mother and says things like, I think I have breast cancer my boobs have been hurting for days, or, I might have a yeast infection but it's not really burning it's different I don't know what else could it be? And the mother says soothing things like, you don't have breast cancer and

"Cells that wire together fire together" is something the daughter reads about the way memories are formed. In depression the hippocampus shrinks preventing the wiring-together, which prevents the memory forming and

This is something to celebrate. The mother has hired a limo. The daughter is one of the big kids graduating from the sixth grade. The ceremony is happening on the blacktop next to the tetherball pole and it's hot out here. The limo is idling beside the playground. The limo will take the sixth grade to a pool party after the ceremony. This is the last day the mother will be the daughter's teacher. The mother the principal is speaking at the podium. The teachers are handing out paper achievement awards. The daughter has a fever and can't stand in line to receive her paper achievement award. The daughter is nauseous and sweating. The mother is sweating. The father is taking photos. The chalked four square court erases under the parents' folding chairs. The daughter will be lifted into the limo because she doesn't want to miss anything and

The daughter repeats the fever at her high school graduation and at her college graduation, where during the ceremony she lies with her head in her roommate's lap. All week the daughter has been wandering around Davis Square filling out applications in all the restaurants and eating ice cream cones one after another while the mother has been packing up the house in which the daughter's childhood took place. This is how the daughter thinks of it. Next week the mother is moving to Vermont and the daughter will, with any luck, be a waitress. The daughter's black gown is sticking between her legs. The father wants to take a photo with the daughter. Something for his new house. Please, the father says. He wants her to put on her mortarboard. The daughter imagines the photo on the father's new mantelpiece, if the father has a mantelpiece. You don't like change, the mother says, so you always get the flu or

The mother tells the daughter she must write her college admissions essay. This is not up for debate. This is junior year of high school, for Christ's sake, this is what everyone's doing. The daughter is lying on the deck in her bathing suit and she's not taking her sunglasses off. She refuses to go to college. She refuses to think about college. She refuses to visit the guidance counselor to talk about college admissions and she definitely refuses to write a college admissions essay. This should be the goddamn easy part, the mother says. Either the daughter will write an essay about graduating from sixth grade or

The daughter gets a job as a waitress in Davis Square and she gets a job in a cubicle in Post Office Square, and it's outside this job, on her lunch break, while she's sitting on the steps eating her sandwich, that the father calls and says, you'll never be able to support yourself, you'll never have anything without me. After that the daughter uses the nice paper in the office to print grad school applications and when she gets into grad school she gets a job as a waitress in Virginia and after that she gets a job adjuncting at a university and a new job as a waitress in a fancy restaurant where some Dallas Cowboys come in and tip her $300 and she does all this thinking, you can go fuck yourself or

The mother and the daughter are breaking into the father's office. Though technically they're not breaking in: The mother has a key. The daughter has driven from college and the mother has driven from the house where childhood took place. This is how the daughter thinks of it. The father is stealing the mother's money: Because the mother is sure the daughter is sure. They've agreed they need to find out what the father is doing before whatever the father is doing is done. Before the separation becomes a divorce and the divorce is final and the mother can't pay the mortgage on the house where childhood took place. They've parked next to each other in the empty parking lot, far away from the pools of overhead lights, like criminals or

The mother half-listens to the directions and she's heading off across the quad. New students have received college admissions packets and are directed to freshman dormitories. The daughter trails the mother who's carrying the comforter and the mattress pad she'll unfurl on the twin mattress while the daughter sits on the linoleum and rips her name tag into little pieces. Are you really leaving me here or

The hallways are dark. There is no security guard at the high reception desk, no security guard roaming around with a flashlight like in the movies. The elevator buttons work exactly like they do in the daytime and when the doors open on the second floor it's a short walk to the father's office. It feels like the middle of the night and

The daughter finds her college admissions essay in a plastic bin in the mother's basement in Vermont, where the daughter is spending her thirty-eighth birthday. The essay, which she didn't remember, is about her sixth-grade graduation and contains a memory within a memory: "I thought back to when I was in preschool. I was surrounded by my friends but only wanted to be with my mother who taught at the other end of the building. I would walk down the deserted hallway, listen to the tap of my shoes on the linoleum, until finally I found her classroom. While she taught I played with the paper clips and pencils in my mother's drawers." Was the daughter walking or was she running, as she remembers now? Was she being chased or

The writing must hold the feeling of the memory, the daughter tells her students, and

The father doesn't appear in the daughter's college admissions essay. The daughter's feeling that she'll never be so close to the mother again is a bit on the nose, but here is the four square court and here is the tetherball pole. Either the daughter will use these details or

Parking lot, elevator, dark hallway. The daughter has tried to write the breaking-into-the-office story in many different ways in many different years but she finds few details in her memory. Just excitement, ickiness, dread. Either she'll stop trying or

Find a way to capture those feelings in images, the daughter tells her students. How? they want to know. Every time you see an abstraction, erase it. And then what? they want to know. Who knows, no one knows. Invent an image and

The daughter is standing at the door of the father's office. The daughter is sweating. The mother has a key that fits this lock. The daughter might have a fever. This isn't breaking and entering because there will be no breaking. They will find out tonight what the father has stolen from the mother and

The daughter's college graduation photo never shows up on the father's new mantelpiece, or it shows up but then he takes it down, or there is no mantelpiece. The daughter is only in his new house because the father's dead and she doesn't remember to look for a mantelpiece, and she's not remembering her college graduation, and the only photo she'll remember seeing later is a framed 8 × 10 of the father. A headshot he took for his business cards, she'll find out. She'll remember seeing the headshot displayed on the piano, but no, there is no piano, the father didn't own a piano. She'll remember seeing a shit-colored, man-sized stain on the white rug and

They either open this door or

Memory can't be trusted, the daughter tells her students. Or memory can be trusted entirely. Or

The daughter is standing over her brother who is under a table and there's some blood and some broken picture frames, and is this a photo of the mother and daughter from which the mother has been razored out or

Are they doing something wrong? Will we be arrested? the daughter asks the mother. The money is ours too, the mother says. Your father is not the only one who works for a living. Should they turn on the lights in here or

The father is moving out of the house where the daughter's childhood took place. She's come home from college and he's come home to take the things he wants. This is how the daughter thinks of it. One of the things he wants is half the photographs but no, not these, these are the cheap frames, why are you trying to give me the goddamn cheap frames? He wants these, the Waterford, the ones his clients gave him, the twentieth-anniversary present, and do they think he cares what's in them? Do they think he wants photographs of this crazy bitch and

Maybe just one lamp? Turn the light on, the mother says. We're not criminals. The mother and the daughter are in the father's filing cabinets. These aren't my signatures, the mother says. What are we looking for? the daughter says. Evidence, the mother says, or

The photographs the father wrangled out of crystal floating down the stairs or

The copy machine flashlighting the wall in a single white streak or

The father throwing the Waterfords in a box without wrapping them or

The mother collecting documents in a box she brought for this purpose or

The daughter standing around with Bubble Wrap or

That's my grandmother's fucking lamp, the mother says, or

The daughter is writing another essay or

Here is the evidence but what if it changes nothing?

Good to Know

To manage an estate, a lawyer will require a retainer of $5,000.

In a will, a man may name anyone he likes to be the personal representative/executor/executrix of his estate.

The retainer is payable upon signature.

A personal representative/executor/executrix is often but not always a family member.

Yes, this means up front.

The last will is the legal document.

No, you may not pay by credit card.

Yes, the money may be borrowed.

At the reading of the will, the named personal representative/executor/executrix may decline to accept responsibility for the estate.

What happens then?

It is not always clear why a man will amend his will in the last weeks of his life but this happens frequently.

Note the addenda.

A signed legal document is binding.

If the named representative declines, the estate passes to the state.

The named representative may accept with or without misgivings.

At the reading of the will, it is not always possible to tell if the estate has an upside-down debt-to-asset ratio.

If the named representative accepts, there are two processes under which she may be instated as the personal representative/executor/executrix of the estate.

What's a debt-to-asset ratio?

One is the informal process and one is the formal process.

It's just what it sounds like.

A funeral director will require a deposit of $3,000 before any services are provided.

The terms "executor" and "executrix" are gendered, and equivalent under the law.

The fee includes all the candy in the crystal bowl and all the pens in the crystal cup.

The formal process requires several months and notices published in newspapers.

Not the crystal cup itself.

No, you may not pay by credit card.

A florist is accustomed to receiving requests for funeral arrangements on short notice.

A personal representative, if she is female, may be referred to as the executrix.

Fees will vary depending on the type of bloom and the complexity of the arrangement.

What about jonquils?

What's an annuity?

Jonquils?

An annuity bypasses the estate and is paid directly to the beneficiary.

It is acceptable though unusual to request pots of yellow jonquils for a funeral.

Most assets must pass through the estate.

A florist will deliver.

An annuity is a kind of life-insurance policy.

A funeral director will require the remaining $3,000 before turning over the cremains.

This business may require a vocabulary lesson.

Sometimes the formal process is necessitated.

Sometimes there are delays at the crematorium.

No, you may not pay by credit card.

The order of the distribution of assets is prescribed by law.

Don't worry, a sample urn may be borrowed for the funeral from the funeral home.

The reasons won't always be clear.

Cremains may be mailed to you.

The sample urn will remain empty and may be displayed by the flower arrangements.

Jonquils, are you sure?

There isn't any choice.

An annuity can be paid out in several ways, such as lump sum or lifetime.

Standard or expedited shipping.

Each payout has different tax obligations.

Cremains come standard in a cardboard box.

The newspaper notices necessitated by the formal process alert potential claimants to the status of the estate.

An urn may be purchased for a fee.

Sometimes a lawyer's retainer will be spent even before an executrix is formally instated by law.

No, you may not pay by credit card.

An urn may be chosen from this display.

Some estates are particularly complex.

Sometimes the beneficiary of an annuity is surprising.

The fee depends on the material and the craftsmanship.

When the retainer has been spent, another payment of $5,000 will be required.

An obituary may be published in a local newspaper but this is not required.

The formal process allows for claimants to make claims against the estate in a timely manner.

A stepdaughter may be the beneficiary of an annuity.

Consider where the urn will be displayed.

Yes, immediately.

Once legally named executrix, the executrix is legally obliged to discharge completely her duty to the estate.

Yes, no matter who receives the annuity.

Credit cards offer advances.

It is acceptable to decline to purchase an urn.

Pay by check.

An estate account should be opened to receive monies in the event monies are paid to the estate even if the estate expects no such monies.

The executrix will be reimbursed for the money she spends and compensated with an hourly salary for the time she spends to discharge her duties to the estate if and only if there are sufficient funds in the estate once the estate settles.

If the IRS makes a claim (or claims) against the estate, the timeline will change.

It's hard to know.

The estate account may be opened in the executrix's home state even if that state is not the same as the deceased's home state.

An official death certificate will be required.

Xeroxes are not acceptable.

Any positive balance is acceptable.

It is acceptable to keep the cremains in the cardboard box on the shelf in a closet.

An official death certificate will be required.

The change may be significant.

A refund from the deceased's cell phone bill prorated after death may be used as a deposit to open the estate account.

An official death certificate will be required.

If the IRS makes a claim (or claims) against the estate in the event that the deceased was being audited at time of death for one (or more) of the preceding tax years, the hiring of an accountant will be necessitated.

An official death certificate will be required.

Consider where the ashes will be spread.

In the case of an IRS claim, it is prudent to contact the deceased's accountant, assuming the deceased and the accountant were on good terms: for example, assuming the deceased had paid his accountant's bill in full.

There will be many discoveries.

An official death certificate will be required.

An official death certificate will be required.

The executrix is responsible for keeping the estate current and in good standing until the estate settles.

In some cases, a lawyer can negotiate a fee structure with an accountant even if the deceased has not paid his accountant's bill in full.

It doesn't matter how long it takes.

You cannot pay by credit card.

It is easy to transplant jonquils from pot to garden.

A time sheet should be kept noting hours and minutes.

An official death certificate will be required.

On the checks issued for the estate account, the executrix's name will be printed beneath the name of the deceased.

Assuming the lawyer has cut his rate from $300/hour to $250/hour, five minutes on the phone answering a question will be billed at $21, rounding to the nearest dollar.

Checks printed in this way will be reminiscent of the checks issued for a first bank account, on which a child's name and a parent's name appear together.

No one knows how long it will take to settle an estate.

You will receive weekly statements.

An estate account will incur a service fee of $25/month.

The executrix is responsible for the mortgage payment on any property.

A familiarity with Excel is useful.

Sell a car immediately so that the estate has a positive cash flow.

An official death certificate will be required.

If there are insufficient funds in the estate account to pay the service fee, the account may be overdrawn.

An initial positive cash flow may be used to hire a Realtor, clean out a house, or engage an auctioneer.

An auctioneer?

Talk fast and write everything down.

Cars depreciate quickly.

1-800-GOT-JUNK is a useful and expensive service.

No property of value may be removed from the house by family members; all material assets belong to the estate and must be cataloged and liquidated.

The sale of a car does not usually result in a large influx of cash.

In the case of a home office, a professional shredder must be hired.

A case may be made for photo albums as they have no monetary value.

If the estate account is overdrawn, the executrix may pay the service fee from her own account.

If a deceased's ex-girlfriend-now-friend cuts the door off the deceased's safe before the arrival of the family, it is best not to think about this.

If the mortgage is not kept current and the property goes into foreclosure, the executrix may be held legally responsible.

An official death certificate must be resent.

A password on a home computer may or may not be guessed.

A professional shredder may be engaged to come to a house.

Transplant the jonquils at the right latitude at the right time of year.

The truck itself is a shredder!

The job of the executrix is to liquidate all assets in a timely manner and to get money into the hands of the claimants who have legitimate claims on the estate, or for whom provisions have been made in the will, even if the executrix has no such claim or provision.

Don't ask.

No one will know if the deceased had six pairs of cuff links or seven. A paperweight or a business card holder engraved with the deceased's initials will not be missed.

Follow-up questions will be billed at the rate of $250/hour.

Passwords may consist of familiar phrases.

A business card holder slips easily into a pocket.

It is easier and more time efficient to hire an auction house, which will provide one lump-sum payment for the deceased's material possessions of value.

Look up any remaining questions on the internet.

Once the executrix is instated as the executrix, she will stay the executrix.

The bill must be paid at the end of the month.

No, you cannot pay by credit card.

No, there are no other options.

Better guesses come from having more familiarity with the deceased's familiar phrases.

No, this cannot be undone.

A lump-sum payment will always be less than items are worth individually.

If a password cannot be guessed, a home computer may be recycled.

Some problems cannot be solved at this time.

There is no value in the deceased's clothes.

Because timeliness is a factor, certain losses are acceptable.

A tie or a belt will not be missed.

A mortgage company will sometimes offer a grace period in the event of the mortgage-holder's death.

Hire a good cleaning company.

Value and expedience form a ratio.

A cleaning company can remove a stain from a rug.

Ratios are a type of equation suggestive of balance.

A man-sized stain; a white rug.

Clothes may be sent to Goodwill.

Steam cleaning may be effective.

Undershirts?

This loss is acceptable.

The grace period will be short.

An official death certificate will be required.

Some things may only be accomplished in the state in which the deceased resided and/or died.

An executrix will visit a notary on a weekly basis.

Yes, you can pay by credit card!

The balance will be hard to understand.

It is possible to fail to discharge the estate's debts in the legally specified order.

Save every document.

Foreclosure is a tricky business requiring many registered letters.

Both electronic and hard copy.

Make friends with a notary.

Make signatures identical.

Open registered letters as soon as they are received.

If debts are not discharged in the order specified by the law, the executrix becomes liable.

Unopened registered letters may fill a Sterilite bin.

File boxes may be purchased at Target.

Some documents may require Medallion Certifications.

A mortgage company's claim has legal precedence over a credit card company's claim, for example.

Any person or business may be a claimant.

Winter is not a good time to sell a house.

Unopened registered letters may fill more than one file box.

Jonquils do well in full sun.

It is inadvisable to store file boxes of unopened registered letters under a bed.

Many banks have discontinued Medallion Certifications but a bank's corporate headquarters may still provide them.

A Realtor's fee may be paid out of any profits from the sale of the property, if there are profits.

Please hold.

Medallion Certifications are only available to investment account holders.

Are there other options?

A stepdaughter, even one who has been the recipient of an annuity, may make a claim against the estate.

More open houses may be scheduled.

Claimants may feel as though they have not received an appropriate sum of money, due to hardship or alleged misdeeds preceding the death, and in this case they may sue the estate.

Please hold.

A claimant's story may or may not have legal merit.

It is best to have a post office within walking distance.

Some winters have record snowfalls.

It is best to go in person.

Some claimants are litigious.

Where will that much money come from?

Don't worry.

Litigiousness is a matter of public record.

Please hold.

The executrix is responsible for any necessary repairs on the property until the property sells.

In years of record snowfall, open houses are underattended.

An IRS audit is complex and time-consuming.

Roofs are expensive to repair.

If the executrix behaves negligently in discharging her duties, she may be held liable by a claimant.

If there is an encroachment on the property, the timeline will change.

Please hold.

The price may be lowered.

It is often wise to wait.

If a property doesn't sell, it may be taken off the market.

Spring is a better time of year.

Public records will show evidence of a claimant's other legal actions, such as personal injury lawsuits against employers and/or individuals.

An encroachment may be large or small, such as a corner of a neighbor's shed that crosses the property line.

If the transplant has been successful, jonquils will bloom the subsequent spring.

Once the estate is sued by a claimant, there will be two options.

A property may be put back on the market at a lower price.

The first option will require time and money, such as initial and monthly payments for legal fees incurred to dispute a claimant's suit.

Please hold.

A claimant's suit may be brought whether or not it has legal merit.

The second option is called "settling."

What good will that do?

If and when the property sells, any profit may be turned over to the claimant engaged in a suit.

This account has a negative balance.

The profit, if there is a profit, may or may not be enough to settle the claimant's suit.

Two IRS audits are more complex and more time-consuming than one.

A claimant's lawyer will advise his client to accept a settlement if and only if the full value of the estate is equivalent to the profit from the sale of the property, and if and only if the full value is guaranteed to the claimant.

Don't worry.

Bulbs will multiply underground.

This is a resolution.

Most debt holders such as credit card companies, medical insurance companies, utility companies, and hospitals will settle with the estate for pennies on the dollar once it is clear the estate has no value.

Sometimes you get lucky.

Some estates may settle within a year.

Jonquils are annuals and will bloom every spring.

Some estates may remain open six or more years.

An official death certificate will be required.

Don't worry?

Please hold.

This loss is acceptable.

A Wedding in Five Scenes, September 2013

REHEARSAL.

A man is standing in front of a window that looks over a golf course and a sky that looks like rain. Between us, set white tables with folded yellow napkins and empty vases that tomorrow will be filled with flowers. Tomorrow my brother will be married and there will be half-filled glasses and strangers dancing and my nephew will fall asleep under one of these tables. The roses will be yellow and white, and the favors will be miniature bottles of maple syrup. It's Vermont. Man in front of a window. Man looking at the sky. Man who is my father?

Isn't there something familiar about the way the man stands? Is there? Man in an off-white sports coat. Man with colorless hair.

When the man turns around, I say, Dad. And he is.

We are alone in the room with the tables. We might hug. We hug. His smell is not familiar.

Neither of us knows where we're supposed to be. He says, where is Cameron? Your brother? Where is Cameron?

I don't know.

He says he will see if he can find Cameron. We find the stairs.

I'll go downstairs? he says. Where is Cameron?

Where is anyone. I don't know what to do next so I stand there. This is our reunion. I've been expecting it all summer and here it is. I've been expecting it for ten years and here it is.

Father in an off-white sports coat. Father with colorless hair.

Tomorrow my brother will be married and there will be the champagne and the flowers. We'll unfold our yellow napkins.

Father with colorless hair. Father coming upstairs.

There will be the dancing and the disco ball.

The stairs have been an effort. He holds the end of the rail.

Have you seen Brittany? he says. My daughter?

His gaze is like water over water.

Dad, I say, it's me.

REHEARSAL DINNER.

Father in a car with the heater running. Father in a black Miata. A party tent in a field filled with strangers. Father zipping up his coat. My father rolls down the window halfway. I'm holding a mound of baked beans on a yellow plate. I pass the plate through the opening.

Can I help you get out?

No.

My father rolls up the window. Father with head on the headrest. Father with colorless hair. Father with eyes closed. Now just one second, I have to go cry in my mother's bathroom and then I'll bring out more salad. Oh, more paper cups? OK. The car is what they call a soft top. It's early September. The ground is smoking where the pig was pulled out of a pit. The car at least is familiar. Father with a scarf on? Father opening his eyes. My father rolls down the window halfway. I'm holding a mound of pork on a yellow plate.

The grass isn't very wet.

It isn't?

My father rolls up the window. Father with a scarf on in September. Father with a forkful of pork. Father in a car with the heater running. Black Miata on the edge of the woods. Hold on, I have to go cry in my mother's bathroom and then I'll bring back a cake knife. That's some sun over there, look. Wait, no it isn't. Father with an interior light switched on. Who needs a bottle opener? Here. Father in a car with the heater running. Father with small eyes. My father rolls down the window halfway. I'm holding a piece of white cake on a yellow plate.

The cold is too much for me now. Blood poisoning. Got my wisdom teeth out, now everything else is going downhill. I didn't know if you knew. I've been in the hospital. Oh god it's been terrible. Terrible terrible. It's been, did you know?

Can I get you anything else?

No.

My father rolls up the window. Father eating his cake, good. Dark on the edge of the woods. No, father eating one bite of cake. No, it's just the yellow rose. Hold on, I have to carry leftover beans up to the house and then I'll go cry in my mother's bathroom. We had too many beans, I know! Father in a car with the heater running. Strangers starting up trucks. I brought more Tupperware down, here. A cloud of dust over the field. Water in the coolers. Dead grass in the tent. Someone turn on the house lights so we can see our way back up. Here we are. Yes there's more beer. Serving dishes in the sink and a spoon falling. Father in the car with the heater running. Kidneys failing. Headlights still on the edge of the woods. Who's going down to tell him it's over? The driveway is long and quiet. Liver failing. Father alone in the car on the edge of the woods. Ammonia building up and traveling to the brain.

CEREMONY.

Will he manage the walk to the green? He manages the walk to the green. Will he manage the walk down the aisle? He manages the walk down the aisle. Will he manage to stand for the photographs? He's standing in the photographs. What happened last night? Where did he go? I don't know, I don't know.

RECEPTION.

My father sits beside me. My father stands when I stand. My father sits when I sit. We unfold our yellow napkins. What do we talk about? We talk, but. It's great to see you again too, Dad. Dad sits beside me all night.

BREAKFAST.

These friends from out of town, this family from out of town, breakfast in my mother's kitchen. Eggs, pancakes, take this muffin. Wait, here's the black Miata coming up the driveway. What's he doing, my mother says. Who's going out there?

I will.

I'm standing in the driveway with my father. I didn't know if you knew, he says. I didn't know where you were. I miss you.

The Personal Essay: Round Two

I read some of the personal-essays-in-progress to a friend.

I don't understand the concept of the My-Dead-Father-in-the-Sky-Singing thing, she says.

I try to explain. This goes on for a long time. Finally I say, never mind, I don't understand it either.

Also, she says, "Dad" lightens the tone. You should consider "Father."

Good Dad-in-the-Sky: We need the tone to be lightened. Otherwise, none of us will be able to get anywhere.

Also, she says, I don't really think the coal thing and the widow's walk thing go together. The fact that they're part of the same house isn't enough. It's not clear what anything means. What's the thread? It's all mixed up.

Good Dad-in-the-Sky: You can't change my name now.

I try writing chunky paragraphs with connections and transitions that make sense.

Bad Dead Dad: Better a chunky paragraph than a chunky woman.

Stop it.

Is it enough that they're part of the same family?

When I'm twelve, my father looks at a photo of me and says, better you weren't wearing your retainer. I'm standing on a ski slope, leaning against one of my ski poles and I'm smiling a big smile. I actually sort of like the photo, before this. Usually, I keep my mouth shut.

Too bad about that retainer.

I write three chunky paragraphs about my retainer and my ski poles and then I attempt to connect the story about my father and the photograph. Now I have a solid past tense. In doing this exercise, I learn that a story with connections and a solid past tense would be better. So, too, a story without retainers. A story without Dead Dads?

Don't say that, the Dead Dads say. In fact, maybe you shouldn't say any of this.

I write another two paragraphs about Vermont and the chairlift and how it's spring and the snow is mostly slush so it sprays up and drips down inside our boots and our socks are soaked but we don't care because it's warm it's spring it's the most beautiful day blah blah. Then I go on to discuss how "we" includes my brother, my mother, and me, and how this is a fact of my childhood.

I like the writing but I don't know how anything's connected, my friend says.

Where the father is, I don't know.

I have my mouth shut in every other photograph I can find taken of me between the ages of twelve and twenty-one. After that I opened my mouth only if someone said, why won't you *smile*?

What happens when you have to say something more than once?

I can see that this is a real problem I don't know how to solve.

How about some transitions? she says. How do we get from one thing to another?

What does "related" mean? What does "and then" mean?

She says, I like some of those details though.

Wait, I say, are the Dead Dads singing?

Yunk Sale

Good Dad-in-the-Sky is singing.

It's summer again in the suburbs. It's 1993. In the old neighborhood, it's childhood. On the way to my brother's T-ball game there's a yard sale. Yunk Sale, my father says. We park at the curb beside the boxes of folded clothes. On the center table there are two whistles, some baseball caps, and a model fighter plane my brother might want. Two women in T-shirts are back there in the shadow of the garage, pulling lampshades and cookie tins off the grass. I might want that plane, my brother says. This year he's a Royal and we're all disappointed he isn't a Red Sox. His hair's sticking out long from under the blue cap. My father surveys the area without moving his feet. He pats his flyaway hair flat. Vroom, my brother says with the plane in his hand. We don't know whose plane that was, I loud-whisper. Someone might have *died.*

Yunk Sale, Yunk Sale, get your yunk! my father sings in the car all the way to the game.

This mispronunciation is one of my father's favorite jokes. I can't tell you why.

Realtor sends me the promotional video for my father's house in Marblehead, which is now, legally, my house.

Legally, Bad Dead Dad says.

The video shows me there are three beds, three baths, finished basement with office, attached two-car garage. The kitchen has been "recently updated." A colonial, built 1989, on 0.12 "beautifully landscaped" acres. We'll find a buyer, Realtor says. What do you think of the video?

It's 1989 and my brother is one and a half. All summer he runs around naked in our backyard in Beverly. When he starts to pee, my mother says, run to the garden! and he pees in the flowers. My mother's going to have him potty trained by fall, just wait.

The jonquils start at Easter and once weren't they as tall as me? My father has a green thumb and a driveway full of mulch.

In the video, there's a panoramic view of the 0.12 "beautifully landscaped" acres in Marblehead. There's a lilac bush and two tulips that I can see, but things aren't looking how they might've looked if my father had been keeping things up. For one, most of the bulbs have forced their way out of the beds. They're peeling like onions on top of what's left of the soil. I've seen them in real life but you can't see them in the video. It all just looks like dirt.

Every spring Saturday, starting in April and going on through a whole childhood, my father says, who's going to help me spread this mulch? Then we all hide. I stand in my closet with the light off.

In Realtor's video, there are long shots of all the clean rooms and the "recently updated" kitchen. I recognize the rooms, sort of. Was I in this house once with my father when he was alive? I feel a memory here but I can't remember. It could be my brother's memory.

Bad Dead Dad: Couldn't you have come to see me one more time, before?

Good Dad-in-the-Sky: I wish we could have seen each other again.

Today the Dead Dads are mostly indistinguishable. Sometimes that happens because I've made them up. What did my father say the one time I was with him in his house if I was with him in his house? Where was he standing?

It's all cleaned out; it's just a house. We cleaned out the bedrooms and the closets and the kitchen.

My great-grandmother dies in 1988, the summer my brother arrives. The first day of the yard sale, in which we're selling her things, is rained out. It's the end of the summer and I'm about to be in second grade. My father covers the tables with tarps. I put my head underneath one and look at all the jewelry while the rain whacks my neck. It's not real, my father calls from outside the tarp, it's costume. There's a phoenix and a starburst. On the second day, it's sunny. Yunk Sale! my father says, doing the unveiling. The neighborhood kids come for the plastic necklaces, twenty-five cents apiece. My father says to me, you're in charge. I clink their quarters in a Santa Claus tin while they spin over the grass in my great-grandmother's beads. Mine mine mine, I think. When they get bored of spinning, they pick blackberries off the bushes growing along the house. Get your yunk here, my father calls.

The Dead Dads want to know what I did with my father's things.

Yunk Sale? Good Dad-in-the-Sky asks.

My father, my brother, and I are whizzing around the old Saturday neighborhood where it's 1993 and the T-ball game is about to happen. We follow the neon poster-board signs. YARD SALE THIS WAY →. Lovett Street, Lothrop Street, Ocean Street. Yunk Sale,

Yunk Sale, Yunk Sale. We whiz past the playground with the top down. "Whiz," I say in my head until the word detaches from its meaning. My father's holding his baseball cap on his head. Sky blue, ocean blue, lilac blue. Now we have some things in the trunk my mother won't like. I don't even want my own junk, she says, why would I want anyone else's?

My father and I are whizzing around the old Saturday neighborhood in Beverly where it's 1987 before my brother's born. We're going to Dunkin' Donuts and Star Market and the Italian grocery on Rantoul Street whose name I can't remember.

What was the name of that grocery? I ask Good Dad-in-the-Sky. I look for it on Yelp.com and on Yellowpages.com and on Googlemaps.com, where it isn't.

We do this every weekend, the way some people go to church or synagogue. My father pulls the car into the parking lot of the grocery on Rantoul Street whose name I can't remember and says, betcha I can get you a cookie. A pink one? Painted on the side of the grocery is a mural of a vineyard. Welcome to eeetaly, my father says in a fake accent. We unbuckle my seat belt and I slide off the seat, which is black and hot where my legs weren't.

I call my brother to find out some information. What was the name of that grocery store on Rantoul Street? I say. The one with the bad mural of the vineyard?

I sort of remember, he says. But he doesn't remember.

The perspective was wrong, going up into the hills? They used to give us those pink Italian cookies. With sprinkles? While we walked around the store?

That was you, he says. Dad and I didn't do that.

My brother has to go because he's driving and his baby is crying in the back seat. I maybe remember the cookies, he says. Which one was Rantoul Street?

He wasn't born then, and then he was little, and then those Saturdays were over. Now we've found today's Sad Thing.

My father buys a pound of rare roast beef, which the big, bearded man who has given me a pink cookie slices lace thin. When we get home, we'll have sandwiches.

It wasn't a Yunk Sale, I say to both Dead Dads. I didn't make poster-board signs or collect change in a Santa Claus tin. I didn't haul any of my father's things out into the yard. I sold what I could, remotely, to a woman in Marblehead with a consignment shop called Dorothy's Lane. Then I hired someone, remotely, to take the rest away.

1-800-GOT-JUNK? Bad Dead Dad wants to know. Did you make any money?

I paid for everything.

Gloria's, my mother says, when I call her. On Rantoul Street. You used to go there with your father for the roast beef.

All the leaves in Vermont are apparently changing on the trees and I'm missing them in California.

I make up a sandwich for Good Dad-in-the-Sky.

The Last Time I Saw My Father Alive

Was in a hospital in Holyoke, Massachusetts. Was after he was taken by police. Was after he was taken by ambulance. Was the same day. Was a day later. I knew he was sick but not that sick. Was after state police found him disoriented in his car on the side of the highway. Was just after Thanksgiving. Was just before. Was after local police found him disoriented at a red light. Was after the light turned green. Was after the car was blocking traffic. Was after someone called 911. There hadn't been an accident. He was disoriented. He didn't know where he was. He didn't know who he was. Was after ammonia built up in his brain. Was before I thought much about the word "disoriented." Was after police were on the phone to my brother. Was after a doctor was on the phone to my brother. Was a courtesy. Was a kindness. Was a legal obligation. Was after a nurse tracked down my brother's number. Was before I thought much about medical databases with emergency contact numbers and we were next of kin. Was after my brother called me. We didn't know what was happening. He was there; he was disoriented. Was after a game of telephone. Was after my brother said, we have to. My brother, at least, was next of kin. I was thinking, what happens when someone has no family. He was disoriented; he was scared. Was after a drive in my brother's truck. Was after a snowstorm. Was before I knew ammonia in the brain was a symptom of liver failure. Was before I knew ammonia in the brain was a symptom of kidney failure. I knew he was sick but not that sick. I hadn't learned to spell the word "cirrhosis." I hadn't learned to spell the related word "sclerosis," a hardening. Was after we'd started speaking again. Was after ten years. Was after two phone calls and a family wedding. He'd said, do you know my daughter? Was before I learned liver failure could look like dementia. Was after I'd been hiding. Was after I'd gone West and come back East. I was still hiding. Was after I lied about where I was living. Was after a snowstorm. Was after a satellite parking lot and my brother turned off the engine. Was after I said, do we have to? and my brother said, yes. It was cold outside. It was breathe-in-your-mittens weather. It was good to be thinking about weather. Was after which wing? Was after which floor, which unit, which room? Was after an elevator ride. I said, can we get a beer after this? My brother said, can we get a beer before this? and thank god we laughed. Was after a walk down a hallway. It was all familiar. Was after a walk past a nurses' station. He was in the bed. He was disoriented. He was agitated. The gown rode up over his legs. His penis came out below the gown. The penis was wearing a condom. Was before I connected condom and catheter. Was before I knew anything about ammonia. Was when I still thought ammonia was a cleaning fluid. I looked away. I didn't look. There was a mess on the floor. I thought what I was seeing was blood poisoning. I thought what I was seeing was the result of wisdom teeth extraction. I still believed what my father told me. Was in the greenish hospital light we all know. He was agitated. He was trying to get out of bed. The nurse said, we need to stay in bed. The nurse said, Bob. The nurse spoke like a mother to a toddler. There were sheets and towels and gloves and gowns and fluid maybe urine on the floor. He didn't know who he was. He didn't know who we were. A doctor said a few words. The nurse said a few words. The nurse spoke to us like a mother to a bunch of toddlers. We didn't know why what was happening was happening. I could only believe, blood poisoning. I could only believe, wisdom teeth extraction. The nurse was starting in the middle. The nurse looked at me like I was delusional. The nurse looked at me like I was crazy. The nurse looked at me like, this can't be the daughter. I said, I understand. I said, thank you. I knew he was sick but not that sick. The nurse said, we're moving him out of the ICU. The nurse said, we're moving him upstairs. We waited. We were familiar. Was after we waited a long time. Was after chairs were brought in and chairs were removed. The condom was removed. The cannula was removed. The gown was set right. The sheet was set right. Was after a slide to the elevator. Was after his hand dropped through a bed rail. I said, stop you'll break it. Was after the hand was set right. Was after a hallway. Was at a window. There was a parking lot out there. There was snow on the ground out there. There was the clean floor. Was after he started to come around. Was after he said, I'm cold. Was after he said, can I have some tea? Was after I put the Patriots on TV. Was before I thought much about the phrase, "drank himself to death." The nurse said, no dear, not right now. Was after I said, can we have another blanket? He said, Brit, please. I said, we need another blanket. Was after he recognized me. Was after he recognized my brother. I was thinking, how long do we have to stay. I was thinking, my father doesn't drink tea. He said, tea. I thought, can't. I said, not right now. I said, in a little while. I said, we can only stay a little while. Was after he said, will you come back? I looked at the parking lot. I looked at the snow. I knew he was sick. Was after I said yes. Was before I meant no.

Enough's Enough

Did my father know he was going to die? Did I know my father was going to die? I want to know other things but right now I want to know this.

These are not questions for the Dead Dads. They are like God in this matter: nonexistent. Which is to say, no help.

It's March 17, 2014, my father's sixty-third birthday; next month he'll be dead. I'm in the study of a borrowed house in Lenox, Massachusetts. This will be the last time I speak to my father but I don't know that yet. I want to call him on his birthday but I agonize all day. I carry the phone everywhere and then I carry the phone into the study and now it's nighttime. My father doesn't know I'm in his state or in his time zone. We will both be speaking in the dark. I look out the windows at the dirty snow lit by a porch light.

We say hello. I speak in a loud voice. Dad *Dad* DAD. It's me, Brittany. After a few tries he knows it's me. Relief. His voice sounds more familiar now. I assume he assumes I'm in California. If he assumes anything. If he remembers anything. I don't say anything to contradict what he might remember or assume. As though if he finds out I'm in Massachusetts he might drive across the state and show up on this doorstep.

There was a time he might have driven across the state. There was a time he would have shown up on the doorstep.

I never learned to tell that time from this time.

That's why if he says, how's California? I will say, it's beautiful.

I never stopped being afraid of my father.

What he says is, when I feel better I'm going down to Florida to look at some places.

I say, I think that's a great idea.

He says, I can't take the cold anymore.

I say, no more winter.

I think he might move to Florida. I also think we're talking about Florida because he's going to die.

He knows it and I know it?

None of my knowing has changed my actions. The only thing that's changed is my thinking about my actions. There have been many days I have said out loud, he's going to die, he's going to die, HE'S GOING TO DIE. Then I carry the phone in and out of every room but I can't call his number.

Maybe none of us believes we will die because the only experiential evidence we have suggests the body will save us. This is true until the moment it isn't, which is the moment of death. Seeing my father's body before, during, and after his death makes me think of my death in a new way. Now I have some new experiential evidence and this is the closest I have ever felt to death.

It is also the closest I have ever felt to my father.

My father says, Florida, it's always warm.

I say, you're moving to Florida. You'll never have to deal with snow again.

I'm going down to Florida and you'll visit me?

Yes, I say, and mean it.

My Father's Dying And

I'm teaching this night class for adults on contemporary San Francisco poets. My father's dying and someone's asking me if this poem's a sonnet. My father's dying or already dead. My father's dying and why didn't I cancel class? My father's dying and I teach every one of my classes even this night class and after that I finally show up at the airport. Yes I could've gotten an earlier flight. My father's dying and there are a lot of debts but I don't know that yet. My father's dying and I'm going to be his executrix but I don't know that yet. My father's dying and his stepdaughter who works at the Crazy Chicken is going to sue the estate and the estate is going to mean me but I definitely do not know that yet. My father's dying and the Crazy Chicken is what my father called the White Hen Pantry. My father's dying and it's too late to correct anything. The White Hen Pantry went out of business years ago. My father's dying and he used to take me to Dunkin' Donuts on Saturday mornings where I used to get a chocolate-coconut. My father's dying and I'm at SFO and I don't remember much of that. My father's dying and I'm flying a red-eye that's all I know. My father's dying and do I feel like I have some special status flying last minute toward my dying father? Yes. My father's dying and everyone's father dies. Yes they do. My father's dying and everyone's sleeping. My father's dying and am I congratulating myself on making this trip across country? My father's dying and this guy's not sleeping, he's watching *The Hangover Part III*. My father's dying and I'm watching *The Hangover Part III*. I put in my earphones and I'm listening. My father's dying and now I often get chocolate-coconuts and I'd like a chocolate-coconut now and is this plane already landing? My father's dying and here I am and in that I have succeeded. It's morning. My father's dying so we probably have to rethink the word "succeed." My father's dying and I'm in Logan and it's familiar even though I don't recognize anything. My father's dying and he's getting off every plane. My father's dying and for a long time he'll be driving every car and riding every bus but I don't know that yet. My father's dying and he's coming out of the men's room. My father's dying and people are walking around here without their shoes. My father's dying without his shoes. No that's not him being searched. My father's dying and there he is standing in line at Dunkin'. Any minute he might turn around. My father's dying and any minute he might call me. My father's dying and he's the only one of us who says my name using three syllables. My father's dying and maybe he didn't get tired of all the syllables because he said my name so infrequently. I got tired. My father's dying and he liked to stretch out my name in his mouth, isn't that romantic? My father's dying and is it important to remember now that I hated the way he said my name? No. Is it important to think about that tone of voice? No. Is it important to remember that tone at all? No forget it. My father's dying and now I can only hear my name said correctly by strangers in Italy or France or when I scan it for my students and is that fair? BRIT-tan-y. What is that? I say. And they say, it's a dactyl. My father's dying and I'll wait in line at this Dunkin' in Terminal B, saying my name like a dactyl. The line is enormous. If your father's dying you should get to cut the line. Move over. My father's dying so no more black coffee for him. No more Crazy Chicken cup no more Dunkin' Donuts cup when it was still paper before everyone went Styrofoam then paper then Styrofoam again. Never mind about the landfills. My father's dying and am I still waiting in line when my mother and my brother and my brother's wife and my brother's kid are all out there at the curb? My father's dying and who cares, give me the Styrofoam. Do I really want to stop and feel grown up for paying for the expensive-as-shit last-minute red-eye and getting myself this coffee so I wouldn't be a zombie when I go pull the plug? Is "zombie" really a word you want to use right now? No. My father's dying and I'm managing my rolly bag and my shoulder bag and this coffee through the revolving door like a champ. My father's dying and is it OK or not OK to say "pull the plug"? My father's dying and I'm repeating pull the plug pull the plug pull the plug all the way through this revolving door. My father's dying and I'm standing on the curb. My father's dying and I'm thinking about a shower. My father's dying and is it OK to think about a shower on the way to pull a plug? My father's dying and here's my brother putting my bag in the truck bed. Hello hello. Can you believe this? We cannot believe this. My father's dying and we must go directly. We must go directly to pull the plug. My father's dying and now there's only one quick car ride left. My father's dying and under the harbor we go. Under the ground we go. My father's dying and Mass General is the place of some bad memories for all of us and let's not think about that. And how the cold wind does blow. My father's dying and some of us are about to make another bad memory and is that fair? It stings your toes and bites your nose and oh here we are in the parking garage. My father's dying and for years I had nightmares about whatever's happening inside those revolving doors. My father's dying in there but my brother did not die in there. Just remember that for a minute OK? That was twelve years ago OK? Remember that. My father's dying and I know exactly how much this parking garage used to cost and look how much it is now. Rip-off, my brother says. My father's dying and my brother's driving the truck up and up. Now thirty dollars is fifty dollars. People are sick in there and is fifty dollars fair? No. This parking garage should be paying us. People are dying. My father's dying and one night twelve years ago he paid for my parking. Yes I remember that. Sure I had a credit card. This is one of the best memories I have of my father. My father is dying and I want to remember it.

It's fall it's getting dark. It's late afternoon it's winter. I come out he's going in we're both coming out. It's already dark it's dusk it's almost morning. My brother is maybe dying in there his son is maybe dying in there. It's getting light it's not quite light it's already daylight it's morning. My father approaches me I approach my father my father and I come outside together through the revolving doors. Here's forty dollars. Here's his wallet here's my hand his hand he holds out the money. I take it. The day is better he says the day is worse I say you'll see when you get in there you'll see what I mean. My father is just arriving I've been here all night I'm just arriving. My father and I are leaving together. We're in the garage. We're riding the elevator. We're side by side looking straight ahead. We're parked on different floors and one of us is getting off first. We're saying goodbye goodbye. We're hugging we never touch. We say I love you we say nothing.

I Work on Banishing the Dead Dads Because the Book Is Written

Good Dad-in-the-Sky: If she doesn't believe in heaven or hell or the River Styx or reincarnation or the Great Big Energy That Knows Everything, and she doesn't believe her father is anywhere as the he-himself

Bad Dead Dad: we're all she has.

Good Dad-in-the-Sky: Why are we in San Francisco?

Bad Dead Dad: She made us cross the country so she can banish us. And now she's sleeping through it.

Good Dad-in-the-Sky: It's only fair. She always came to us.

Bad Dead Dad: If she'd visited her father more often, we wouldn't be here.

Good Dad-in-the-Sky: Remember driving cross-country when she was a kid?

Bad Dad Dead: Not as far as Californ-eye-ay.

Good Dad-in-the-Sky: Vegas, baby.

Bad Dead Dad: She won a carful of stuffed animals while her father lost money.

Good Dad-in-the-Sky: There was a woman on a trapeze flying across the ceiling and a woman in a cage who turned into an ape.

Bad Dead Dad: Why doesn't she write about that?

Good Dad-in-the-Sky: A trick of the light.

Bad Dead Dad: Why doesn't she write about all the times her father took her to the Ice Capades? Remember all the times he would throw her in the air and she would somersault into the pool?

Good Dad-in-the-Sky: Most of her memories are happy memories.

Bad Dead Dad: Look at the bookshelves in here. No one needs all this poetry.

Good Dad-in-the-Sky: Look at her sleeping.

Bad Dead Dad: Or all this dust.

Good Dad-in-the-Sky: She looks tired.

Bad Dead Dad: She looks older

Good Dad-in-the-Sky: but I can picture her little.

Bad Dead Dad: Will she just stop talking to us like she stopped talking to her father?

Good Dad-in-the-Sky: She needs us, we're here. She doesn't need us, she forgets us.

Bad Dead Dad: That's some bullshit. On the other hand, we don't need her. We're here, aren't we?

Good Dad-in-the-Sky: She's not trying to forget us.

Bad Dead Dad: She made us up to write the book and the book is written.

Good Dad-in-the-Sky: Any last words?

Bad Dead Dad: Good luck, sweetheart.

Good Dad-in-the-Sky: "Our meeting, this evening, is about to end. The story I promised you is in your memory."

Bad Dead Dad: Pretentious.

Good Dad-in-the-Sky: Edmond Jabès.

Bad Dead Dad: Let's blow this popsicle stand. I'm starving. Fried clams?

Good Dad-in-the-Sky: Wintergreen popcorn bars?

Bad Dead Dad: She's remembering Salem Willows.

Good Dad-in-the-Sky: She's remembering going to the arcade a couple of months ago

Bad Dead Dad: the first time in years

Good Dad-in-the-Sky: standing outside and looking across the harbor toward the house where childhood took place. She could see the beach at the end of the street.

Bad Dead Dad: She and her brother talked about spreading their father's ashes there

Good Dad-in-the-Sky: but decided not to.

Bad Dead Dad: Her brother said he was getting used to having them above him in the closet while he worked.

Good Dad-in-the-Sky: So they walked to the end of the parking lot and got the popcorn bars

Bad Dad Dead: Pepto-Bismol pink

Good Dad-in-the-Sky: and the rest of the family thought they were disgusting.

Bad Dead Dad: Someone said, like toothpaste.

Good Dad-in-the-Sky: Even the kids wouldn't eat them. But she still thought they were great.

Bad Dead Dad: And her brother still thought they were great.

Good Dad-in-the-Sky: She's remembering now how her father—these are some of her earliest memories—used to take her there on Friday afternoons

Bad Dead Dad: which he took off from work because her mother thought it was important they spend time together

Good Dad-in-the-Sky: or because he wanted to. We don't know for sure.

Bad Dead Dad: They played Skee-Ball until she won enough tickets to buy wax lips or a red Ring Pop or candy cigarettes, which her mother wouldn't let her have.

Good Dad-in-the-Sky: It's a complicated memory.

Bad Dead Dad: She was afraid to go with him.

Good Dad-in-the-Sky: But she was happy too.

Temperate Asia, Marshlands, or the Mesoamerican Cloud Forest

I find out my father is dead while I'm taking photos in the Botanical Garden.

San Francisco has started charging most people an entrance fee but I have a license saying, this is where I live. My love and I can come to the Botanical Garden any time.

I'm taking close-ups of white flowers with white centers, which are growing on trees so grown together they're one tree here on the edge of the Redwood Grove, the most-well-trafficked part of the Botanical Garden. I have a new phone with a camera. It's the prettiest day and the flowers are coming out beautifully in good light: bright, late afternoon, spring, etc. The flowers are the puffs in the compacts of old-fashioned ladies, see? The Botanical Garden grows things like this on trees.

I'm waiting for a call from my brother. He is going to answer certain questions like, is my father dying?, or, is my father dead?, or, is it correct to say that my father is technically dead but alive?, or dead but technically alive?, etc.

I'm not used to having a camera that takes this sort of pictures.

My brother is driving from Vermont to Boston. Or, he has made the drive overnight. He has been in the hospital all along or he is returning to the hospital to find out these certain things. Because for me it is late afternoon, for him it is already night. For my father it is already neither.

The white is coming out like it's lit from behind, each petal a tiny light bulb, Georgia O'Keeffe white. I'm cupping my hand around the screen.

My brother's call is going to come in a few minutes in the marshlands.

My love and I come together down the slope away from the Redwood Grove until we're at the edge of something that seems to be a miniature estuary. Knee-high golden grasses, egret, brackish tang, etc. But there is no sea in the Botanical Garden.

A man and a woman in safari hats hurry away over a footbridge because we've disturbed their romantic moment, or bird-watching.

I write down the name of the white flower, including its Latin name, in a notebook, which I won't be able to find.

Maybe we're in Africa. Maybe this is a grassland not a marshland. The Botanical Garden is ordered like that, by continent and country. You're only in California in the Redwood Grove.

We sit on a bench with a snarl of hedge forming a half shell over our heads, like we're in a car on a carnival ride and things are about to get fast and fun. We debate if we're in Africa or—

To write about this, I have to Google the Botanical Garden so I'll know which continents are possible and which continent to choose. The map at the top of my search page locates the Botanical Garden, with a purple teardrop, ten miles off the coast of San Francisco in the Pacific Ocean. Maybe there is a sea in the Botanical Garden after all, or a botanical garden in the sea. But this doesn't help me.

We sit in the grassland-marshland waiting for my phone to ring, or my phone rings so we sit down on the bench.

According to the map of the garden, I can see now we're in Temperate Asia or the Mesoamerican Cloud Forest. But this feels neither like forest nor cloud and what does temperate Asia feel like? Right now, I'm having a hard time with the map; it all seems impossible.

We sit in Temperate Asia/marshland/Mesoamerican Cloud Forest and I hold the phone.

My brother is in his night alone.

Maybe I am in the sea.

For a few minutes my brother speaks and my father is dead though technically, yes, he is still alive. Then goodbye, goodbye; there are certain things we each still have to do. For one of us this thing will be dying all the way.

On the other side of Temperate Asia, the safari hats stop to listen.

The egret stands still.

On our bench in marshland or Cloud Forest my love and I look at the photographs. We agree to be astonished. And the fancy phone was worthwhile after all. Then we sort out some logistical things like, when will I fly?, and shouldn't someone stay to host the houseguests because, after all, they have a baby and where in the city will they stay, everything's so expensive. All of this is fairly comforting. My love will meet our friends, I will pack a bag, my brother will wait beside the bed where the machines will whir and all night my father will still be alive.

Let's walk home. We follow the safari hats through several countries but all the birds are California birds.